AGAINST THE ODDS

The Memoir Of A Weird Year

Jon Courtenay

*To Richard
Best wishes*

Chapters	Page
1. Audition	3
2. The First Semi-Final Song	22
3. Because Of A Bat: Into Hell	25
4. Lockdown	32
5. Live TV	44
6. The Studio	49
7. The Semi-Finals	53
8. Diagnosis	65
9. The Final	81
10. Champion	90
11. Delay	98
Photos	101
12. The No-Royal, No-Audience, Variety Show. Part 1	105
13. More Delays & Diazepam	121
14. The No-Royal, No-Audience, Variety Show. Part 2	128
15. Skin Graft	135
16. A New Year	149
17. Tumour Two	155
18. Saturday Night Takeaway	172
19. Awards Show	178
20. Belt And Braces	185
Appendix: Against The Odds. The One-Man Musical	188
Acknowledgements	215

Chapter 1
Audition
January 2020

Isn't the most boring part of any autobiography often the beginning? 'Celebs' tell you about their childhoods and family holidays and pet dogs or Grandmas that died and left them heartbroken. All that regular stuff that happens to even lesser mortals not just celebrities, when all you want to read about is the gossip, VIP parties and the truth about the Daily Mail headlines you read in years gone by? This is not an autobiography, it's more a memoir which sounds far more pretentious, but I shall still skip the dead dogs and elderly relatives and start with the headlines. Honestly, I've not had that many. A few local papers ran with 'Local Boy Wins BGT' and then later there were a couple of 'BGT Winner Secretly Battling Cancer' sidelines but I think I came to the party a little late to be falling out of nightclubs or crotchless shots getting out of a limo. If I'm wearing a dress I undoubtedly remember my underwear. Sorry to disappoint.

So I will start as far back as may be interesting, forgoing the early years of loving parents, two weeks every year in Mallorca and not a sniff of abuse save a few dodgy experiences at a boy's boarding school. Maybe we'll come back to that later.

I was forty-seven when I auditioned for Britain's Got Talent in 2020 having been performing since I was a teenager. I watched my parents on stage growing up and knew I wanted to be up there and not sit in the audience. To this day I have never been to a stadium concert, except for Robbie Williams at the MEN where my drunk Sister-in-law turned to the rows behind us and announced that I'd met Robbie and was good friends with his Dad. No one gave a shit except me who was sober and mortified.

When BGT came on the scene in 2007, it was on the heels of other talent shows such as Opportunity Knocks and New Faces, both of which had been hugely successful for many household names that I grew up enjoying on prime-time TV in the 1970s and 80s. Freddie Starr, Paul Daniels, Les Dawson, Frank Carson, Joe Pasquale, Lenny Henry, Victoria Wood and many more. Lee Evans auditioned in 1986 but was rejected and didn't make it past the first audition. Proof that TV talent shows aren't always a good judge of talent. I remember watching those shows with my parents and even managed to get myself an audition for Bob Says Opportunity Knocks when I was fourteen. I was quite concerned that the video of that audition would be unearthed during my BGT experience as it was pretty excruciating. It was the first time that I'd had the idea to combine my talent as a pianist with my love of magic which I had been quite obsessed with since the age of seven. I had rehearsed a three-minute routine at a grand piano where the occasional wrong note would be explained by me pulling a magic prop from inside the piano. Firstly a length of rope, then a snooker ball, then a silk scarf. As each item was removed I would perform a trick with it. On paper, it sounds like it has potential and it may have done if I hadn't arrived at the studio for my audition to be confronted with an upright piano. I had made pockets with cloth and wire that were custom-made to fit around the edge of a grand piano to hold all the props and there was no way they were going to be able to be adapted for an upright piano. At least that's my excuse for my performance; combined with nerves, a lack of experience and a floppy, blonde quiff that kept falling in my eyes, I never stood a chance. I got a very polite letter a couple of weeks later telling me I had been unsuccessful in my attempt to get on the show but please try again in the future. I decided to wait until I was bald.

Simon Cowell took the idea of a talent show and turned it into a television juggernaut with intense editing, behind-the-scenes clips, back stories and a huge budget. It became more of a TV show than a talent show and that was my go-to excuse for not doing it whenever I was asked. There was also a time when Simon would criticise an act as being 'good enough for a cruise ship but not TV' and at the time most of my income was from the cruises. They have come a long way since my world cruise on the famous QE2 in 1997 and now companies such as Disney, Celebrity, Royal Caribbean and many more offer holidays for all ages and budgets with phenomenal entertainment. Cirque Du Soleil and huge west-end and Broadway shows can be seen on board many of these floating cities boasting the latest technological theatres rivalling any on land. I was busy and although I was spending a lot of time away from home, I was making a good living doing something I was passionate about. Why would I put myself out there to be judged by Simon or anyone else and risk being told I was 'only good enough for cruise ships'?

It was September 2019 when I was performing on a ship with a fellow entertainer and close friend, Jamie Allan when he asked me why I hadn't been on the show. Jamie is one of the country's leading magicians with West End shows and hugely successful tours to his name as the iMagician. We had known each other since we were in our twenties when I was still performing a comedy magic act but had never worked together. When I dropped the magic routines from my show and concentrated on the comedy and music I was suddenly working with magicians whose names I had only seen on billings as we passed each other at venues. Jamie and I became good friends. He had some experience with both Britain and America's Got Talent and he was convinced that the show could be a good platform for me.

"I don't know what I can do in three minutes. I play the piano, I do comedy, I sing and I write original songs and parodies. It's tough to put that across in three minutes."

"Why don't you write an original, comedy song and make it about auditioning for BGT?"

"That would never work," I told him.

But the seed was planted and that night I wrote the first version of my audition song which wasn't too different from the version I finally performed at the London Palladium two months later. I played it for Jamie the next day who was excited and thought it would work well on the show.

When I got home I casually announced to my wife Emmah that I was going to audition for Britain's Got Talent and her response was a nonchalant 'That's great babes'. To be fair, I have a habit of announcing big plans which often don't come to fruition and it wasn't until I played her the song that she realised I might have thought this through further than waking up after a lucid dream of an idea. My boys Nathan and Alfie immediately asked if they could come and if they did would they get to meet Ant and Dec? They had quickly prioritised their reasons for being there. I was somewhere below the Geordie duo, Alfie's favourite author David Walliams, Simon because he's Simon and probably Amanda and Alesha because Nathan is a red-blooded teenager.

Emmah gave me a few very valid suggestions for the lyrics of the song and I eventually sent a rough recording of it to my friend Russ Stevens, who is BGT's magic go-to guy and helps to produce many of the magicians on the show. He called me the next day and was very excited. He'd played the song for a senior producer who asked if I would come and audition for the show when they were holding auditions at The Lowry in Manchester, just thirty minutes from my house. My response was immediate:

"It has to be the Palladium. I'm nearly fifty. How else am I going to get an opportunity to appear on that iconic stage with such an incredible history?"

I'm often asked why I waited until the fifteenth season to audition for the show and other than my kids bugging me about it, it was the opportunity to perform at The Palladium. You can see the emotion in my audition. It was completely overwhelming to walk out to that audience on a platform that had showcased all my heroes from years gone by including Charlie Chaplin, Nat King Cole, Judy Garland and Sammy Davis Jr. Growing up watching my heroes on Live From The Palladium, it is just the mecca of variety entertainment and I wanted to have a tiny taste of it. My opportunity was scheduled for 27th January 2020, the last day of the London auditions.

Over the years, like many of my friends in this business, I had received emails or messages on social media from television producers telling me they were working on a show and they thought I would be a good fit. These were the talent scouts for BGT. For a while, there was an agreement between a few of us that whenever we got these requests and politely turned them down, we would suggest they contact our friend Jeff Stevenson as we were certain that he would be keen to get involved. Consequently, Jeff, a seasoned pro of many years, would then get bombarded with requests to be on the show. Jeff has enjoyed huge success over the years from being a child star in the original Bugsy Malone film to appearing on Only Fools and Horses as well as his own TV shows. It kept us amused for quite a while when he'd be fuming that these producers just wouldn't take a hint.

A few years earlier I had gotten into a heated online chat with one of these talent scouts when he asked why I wouldn't consider coming on the show. I quoted Simon's comments regarding cruise ship acts over the years but I was assured he had stopped these unfair criticisms recently as most of the professional acts they were contacting were earning their living on the ships. Then there was the risk of just putting yourself out there to be judged as a full-time working pro. What if for any reason the judges didn't like you and you were buzzed off? I was busy and booked up at least a year in advance so I didn't even have time to take off to audition. Our chat went back and forth with me eventually persuading him that I wasn't interested, but my friend Jeff on the other hand...

That all changed when I had a song that I felt could work and I had the enthusiasm of a couple of the producers behind it. It went through a few rewrites with my usual habit of waking in the middle of the night with an additional line or two only to have forgotten them in the morning. I started keeping a small notebook and pen next to me only to struggle in the morning trying to read the scribbles that I'd attempted in the dark. One of those late-night epiphanies was the line "My teenage son said 'ugh, ugh ugh'" after he'd woken me up playing his Xbox in the middle of the night and I'd told him to go to bed. It turned out to be one of the funniest moments of my audition, making Ant and Dec roar with laughter in the wings. Often simply telling the truth can be funny.

Producers on the show also had suggestions including potential copyright issues. I had originally written some words to parody the tune 'I Dreamed A Dream' when I mentioned Susan Boyle but was told they could never get clearance for that. They even asked if I could sing the words 'I had a dream' instead of 'I dreamed a dream' which I agreed to do and then completely forgot about in the actual performance. I did panic the moment I sang it thinking if there was a copyright issue would they have to leave me on the cutting room floor and not even broadcast my audition? That kind of thing can flash through your mind even in the middle of a song. I love Victor Borge's story of playing a Chopin Polonaise with a full symphony orchestra when a fly landed on the piano music stand and he started to wonder, how does a fly land on a ceiling? Does it fly the right way up and then flip over at the last minute or can it actually fly upside down? All while his fingers were negotiating one of the world's greatest compositions. The brain is a marvellous thing.

Another potential copyright issue was with the music from The Greatest Showman that I wanted to use at the end of the song. There is one person on the BGT production team who is in charge of making sure that any music used on the show has been cleared. It's a mammoth task and she had asked weeks earlier that I be prepared to sing the last lines of the song not to the tune of 'This Is Me' but instead to a tune of my own composing in case there was an issue with it. Composers generally don't like it when you mess with their songs. I had reluctantly agreed to this and rehearsed the song with the new tune only to be told fifteen minutes before my audition that they had just got permission from the composer that I could do it! I was to learn that BGT is not averse to very last-minute alterations, sometimes just minutes before broadcast, but more of that in the semi-finals.

I'm getting ahead of myself. It was in January, two weeks before my audition as I was shaving my face and head (over the years the canvas has gradually increased) that I noticed a new mole just above my ear. Always careful not to nick my scalp as it bleeds for ages, I carefully negotiated the new spot. I was performing on board a Royal Caribbean ship at the time with one of my best friends Pete Matthews and when he kicked my arse, again, at table tennis I joked "Well you should be giving me a chance. I probably have cancer," as I told him about my new mole. How we laughed. As soon as I got home I called my doctor and he took one look, the mole was removed and everything was fine.

Wait. No. That's not what happened.

I got home, ignored the new mole and concentrated on rehearsing my song for a talent show. Idiot.

Emmah, Nathan, Alfie and moley me got the train to London on the 27th of January. We had a number to text when we arrived at the Palladium and a lovely girl met us and ushered us through the registration process and straight into the auditorium where we met up with Jo Allen. Jo runs Greenfairy Productions and is the ex-wife of Jamie Allan (note the slightly different surname spellings, purely coincidental). Jo and I had agreed that she would manage me so I wouldn't be beholden to whatever management deals I would be asked to sign during the show. Within minutes we were sat just a few rows back from the stage as they rehearsed a choir. I was told I would be next.

This is a luxury that is afforded to professional acts who appear on the show; not having to audition in front of producers before they decide if you should get the opportunity to audition again in front of the judges and the television cameras. Usually, there's a long line outside the venue of hopefuls who want to appear on the show but may never get further than a small holding room in front of a couple of TV 'people'. I think this is one of the reasons that the show works as entertainment; it isn't just the good acts that are put through, sometimes gladiators who are far from match-fit are sent to the lions just to entertain the crowds. (Cue Russel Crow "Are you not ENTERTAINED?!") They also want to know your back story to see if there's anything they can mine for further entertainment value. I knew all this thanks largely to Jamie's help and advice. I lost track of the number of times I was asked by researchers to talk about my Dad who died in 2013 hoping that I would bring moist eyes to the proceedings to the point where I even told one of them that they may as well stop as I wasn't going to cry!

Before I knew what was happening I was being ushered onto the stage by Alan, the floor manager. I did manage to just take a moment as I stepped onto the stage for the very first time. A couple of years earlier we had been there to see my friend Paul Zerdin in pantomime and during the interval, I had walked to the front just to touch the stage. That's how magical that place feels to me. The view as I looked back into the beautiful auditorium designed by Frank Matcham, was chilling. Thousands of performers had been here and seen this and now I was one of them. I could only imagine how it was going to feel when it was full of people. As it was, I got a thumbs-up from Emmah and my boys and then I ran through my song for the various producers, runners, creatives and cameramen. They laughed in all the right places and asked if my sound was OK. I said everything felt great and that was it, I was done. The piano was wheeled back off stage and the runner who was looking after us escorted us back to the hotel next door. It was all that quick.

    I must mention here that I have read of and been told stories of contestants on the show complaining of being manipulated. Either being told what songs to sing or what to wear or all manner of stage directions, sometimes against their will. I can only speak as I found and tell you that was never the case with me. After my soundcheck, I approached the judge's table where the senior producers were now sitting in place of the very familiar faces who would be there later and asked them about a joke that I was thinking about including in my performance. When I first sat at the piano I wanted to be shuffling the stool as if it wasn't quite in the right place and then call on one of the stage crew who very apologetically would measure the distance from the stool to the piano with a retractable tape measure as I encouraged him to get it to exactly forty-five centimetres, the exact distance that I required it to be to properly perform my song. As he left the stage I would sit on the stool and tuck it back under my legs.

It was a little comedy bit that had been part of my stage show for years and let the audience know that what they were about to see shouldn't be taken too seriously. I mentioned all this to the producers who very clearly explained that it was entirely up to me. If I wanted to do it, it was in. One of them did suggest that the song was very strong on its own but if I wanted to add something of course that was my choice. It's a small point but one that I remember when I'm told by some people how they felt their moment on stage was being manipulated by forces beyond their control.

Once we were next door in the hotel, the waiting began. It had pretty much been taken over by the show and multiple function rooms were being used for various interviews, social media filming and general organising of the hundreds of people who were there. The clips you see on the show of people sitting on flight cases 'backstage' is often the magic of TV and more than likely are actually in a well-dressed but sterile hotel conference room. The main holding area is in one of the larger spaces and interviews are held here with the contestants in the background slightly blurred. Often many of the 'contestants' are crew working on the show bought in to pad out a few empty seats. Emmah and the boys spent the first hour or two snapping photos with some of the familiar props arranged around the room. The giant BGT letters, Union Jack backdrops and the obligatory flight cases while I disappeared occasionally for an Instagram filming session or an interview or two.

There are two shows on each audition day, an afternoon one and an evening one. Audiences are ushered in and out for each show and I kept asking if there was a running order. Plans kept changing but the final decision seemed to be that I was going to be the very last act in the evening show. On paper that meant I wouldn't be on stage until gone ten o'clock. Realistically, it was likely to be nearer eleven. There was no way that Emmah and the boys would last that long on the uncomfortable office chairs in the holding room so I walked up to the hotel reception not expecting for a minute that there would be any rooms available. I was right, no standard rooms just one junior suite left. I handed over my credit card and remember joking with the receptionist that I'd better win the bloody show because this audition day was racking up some serious expenditure.

We set up camp in our very lovely but overpriced accommodation. Emmah took the boys out for lunch but I had been asked to stay around the holding room in case they needed me for more 'bits' to be broadcast on the show. I made a point of telling our runner that we had booked a room at the hotel so should they want to do any interviews with the rest of the family they only had to let me know and I could ring them. That will become pertinent later on in the day.

I was filmed chatting to a couple of other acts including a magician who sat next to me holding a deck of cards, performing some impressive flourishes with them as we talked. He asked me what I was doing in my audition and after I'd told him I said:

"Are you going to be playing the violin?"

He paused, looked down at the cards explained that no, he was not a violinist, he would be doing some card tricks. Moments like that only made the day seem even longer.

A rather memorable moment came when they asked to film some slow-mo footage of me walking underneath the stage. It had been set up to resemble a backstage area and it was almost as much of a thrill to be underneath the Palladium stage as it was to be on top of it. Bruce Forsyth's ashes are interned in the wall so I had the opportunity to pay my respects. Most of the backstage area of the theatre has been renovated, cleaned, painted and sanitised, long before sanitising was a necessity so it was lovely to see parts of the theatre that had remained relatively untouched over the years.

When I came back up to the stage area the afternoon show was just starting and as no one was there to escort me back to the hotel, I wandered into the wings of the theatre, expecting at any moment for a hand to land on my shoulder but it didn't happen. I stood just inches away from the stage hidden behind a black curtain watching Ant and Dec on the other side filming their bits with the contestants before they walked on stage. A few technicians were standing around me, some with headphones, others with clipboards and I smiled if I caught their eye and they smiled back. I couldn't believe that no one was telling me to get out of the way. It was quite surreal to be watching the familiar show from such an unfamiliar position but it reignited my memory of being five years old, backstage at the Gaumont Theatre in Ipswich with my Dad. My Mum was starring in a performance of Annie Get Your Gun and I can still remember so clearly the thrill of being in the wings and seeing the audience from that angle. I felt special and privileged to be there. When the show was over, I met the actor playing Frank Butler who spurns Annie's romantic advances in the show and kicked him in the shins for making my Mum cry on stage. It didn't occur to me in my young mind that Mum's heartbreak at the hands of this evil man didn't faze my Dad at all! It didn't matter, what I had seen on stage had been real.

I am still fascinated by the editing process of these huge television shows. The amount of footage that they film is phenomenal, even just for me, there must have been hours of film on so many cameras. All that footage has to be collated, labelled and then edited into what you see on your TV. I wouldn't know where to begin and I'm a keen video editor hobbyist. On my audition broadcast, they didn't use a single bit of my interviews or backstage footage. None of my chat before or after with Ant and Dec, but there may be a reason for that which we'll come back to.

Now and then I'd call our hotel suite where the boys had their iPads and the TV and were quite happy although they were starting to get a little frustrated, as was Emmah. Nathan and Alfie just wanted to know if they'd be allowed to stand in the wings to watch my audition so they could meet Ant and Dec. Some families are put in the wings and others are sitting in the audience. I hadn't been told anything despite asking a few people. The day was starting to drag.

Finally, at about ten o'clock I was given a one-hour call and we were all escorted backstage. Emmah was told that she and the boys would be sitting in the audience. Two very dejected boys were led away with their Mum, resigning themselves to the fact that despite hanging around for over twelve hours, they would probably never get the chance to meet the hosts of the show. I was left alone again to wander in the wings some more. The show was by now running about an hour late so I wouldn't be on stage until after eleven o'clock and I could tell that people were getting tired. Between filming, Ant and Dec were exhausted having been on their feet and stood in the wings for the whole day. I spotted David Walliams rubbing his eyes and Simon was openly irritable. A comedian was on stage and instead of the allocated three minutes was now into her seventh but it wasn't going well. Perhaps she was hoping that eventually she'd win them over but the comments weren't good and after she left the stage Simon was heard to say "Please tell me there are no more bloody comedians!" I dashed to the other side of the wings where the running order had been posted, worried that I may have been billed as a comedian but it said 'singer', not even 'pianist'. Not the first time a venue had gotten my billing wrong but in this instance, I was pretty relieved. A young guy was standing next to me who I'd seen around during the day, he was a comedian and had been there as long as I had. Someone with a clipboard came running up to him and said his audition was being rescheduled for

Manchester. He was understandably pretty pissed off. I calmed him a little pointing out what Simon had just yelled. It wouldn't be in his best interests to go in front of the judges today.

I hadn't been feeling particularly nervous until now. The day had been so long that my nerves had long ago decided there was nothing to hang around for but now my time was nigh and the butterflies began. I've got friends in this business who have debilitating stage fright and I've never understood how they cope with it. One of them regularly throws up before a performance. I've always felt excited, anticipating what is to come, but like many other performers, the stage is my happy place. I'm more comfortable walking out in front of thousands than I am walking into a party in front of fifty. It's a common trait amongst showbiz folk. We have to be slightly unusual as for most people, public speaking is more of a common fear than death. Jerry Seinfeld pointed out that if that's the case and you're at a funeral, you'd rather be in the box than giving the eulogy. Very strange. But now I was feeling properly nervous. My television experience was limited to a live dating show on a local TV station when I was eighteen with David 'Kid' Jenson. That footage is thankfully lost but now I was about to put myself out there in front of millions, singing an original song that I hadn't had a chance to road-test with an audience prior to this one. What the hell was I thinking?!

One of the crew came over and said I'd be in the wings with Ant and Dec in five minutes. I was quite excited to meet the 'boys'; they had been part of my life on television for over twenty years. Jamie had given me some good advice about the chat before walking on stage and I'm glad I remembered it. Because Ant and Dec would be so familiar to me, I'd feel as if I knew them and they would play on that. They greet you very casually as if you've met before and you feel immediately relaxed around them so you're having a bit of fun with them and feeling very unguarded expecting them to stop at any moment and say "OK, let's record this…" to a nearby cameraman. The truth is, there is a cameraman with a long lens standing quite a distance behind them recording everything from the moment you first meet. It's a very sneaky but effective method for catching those natural moments for anyone not used to being on camera. Thanks to Jamie I was prepared and we had a very funny chat together, none of which was used in the broadcast. I told them I was only auditioning so I could meet them and now I'd done that I could go then turned round to walk away. Part of me wanted to keep walking but instead Ant said:

"Good luck Jon" and gestured to the stage.

"I just walk on?" I asked,

"Yup," said Dec.

So this was the first weird bit. In my whole career, I'd never stepped onto a stage without at least hearing my name first, let alone onto this stage in front of a packed Palladium audience, but on I wandered and on some hidden, miraculous cue and despite the late hour, the audience burst into enthusiastic applause and I felt immediately at home.

I'd realised from watching the show during the day that the chat you have with the judges at the beginning is heavily edited for the TV. It can be quite a long conversation with whichever judge is taking their turn to interview you. Jamie had also suggested that when I walk on I make immediate eye contact with Simon regardless of who began speaking to me so I tried that but he was still chatting to one of the producers when I walked out and didn't even look up and instead Amanda said good evening. I can't remember the whole conversation but I do remember the end when she said good luck and I waited for one of the other judges to speak to me. There was a moment of silence and I realised I was just meant to go and sit at the piano. It was the first laugh I got and then when I sat down and said

"This is bonkers," the place erupted in a laugh far bigger than my comment warranted. Weirdly in the broadcast, you can hear me say the line but there is absolutely no audible laugh from the audience. No idea why they took that out.

And then I was playing and singing my little song. I ad-libbed the line about Simon not smiling and that's when he did for the first time so I relaxed a little bit. The reaction from the audience took me by surprise. Big laughs and applause throughout the song meant I had to edit my timing as I was going along to allow for the welcome interruptions with the biggest reaction to the teenage son 'Ugh ugh ugh'. I saw Ant and Dec lose it at that point. When I finished and jumped up from the piano the strangest thing happened... I got a standing ovation from the audience and the judges.

Now I realise when you watch the show on your telly boxes that you see this happening a lot but from my point of view, it was very discombobulating. I've been performing for over twenty years and a standing ovation is the greatest accolade you can receive from an audience. Americans are very adept at leaping to their feet but we Brits are a lot more hesitant... and when it does happen it's only after I've poured every ounce of my passion into a full evening's show not after just one song that only three minutes earlier I was worried might not get much of a reaction! You can understand how it knocked me off-kilter slightly. Then to top it off as everyone is still clapping and cheering, I see my eldest son running towards me through the audience. What the hell was going on?!

I should take a moment here to explain what happened off-camera and what Emmah explained to me when we got back to the hotel. Firstly, remember this is a well-oiled TV show and the whole crew knows exactly what they're doing so this is by no means detracting from what happened, it's just the magic of TV. A lot of the emotional shots of Alfie watching my performance, which I only got to see when it was broadcast three months later, were predominantly because he was exhausted! We'd all been up since seven o'clock and it had been a busy day. I'm not suggesting that Alfie wasn't completely emotionally involved in my audition but a lot of that eye-rubbing and emotion was purely down to him being tired. Secondly, all three of them had small lapel microphones attached to them when they sat down in the audience to record their reactions but unbeknownst to Emmah, Alfie thought this meant that anything he said would be broadcast to the whole audience and that freaked him out slightly. That may explain why when the audience leapt to their feet and one of the crew standing by my family asked Alfie to run up onto the stage and hug me, instead he had a mild panic attack and curled up on the floor in a ball! Nathan wasn't going to miss his opportunity though and jumped up shouting "I'll go!"

Consequently, there I was on the Palladium stage now hugging my teenage son while the judges all said the loveliest things to me. Then I became even more overwhelmed and very confused when Nathan started shouting "Dad, Dad, you've done it!" And in my profiterole vision (my friend Sam Kane's vocabuleric creation. Whereas 'vocabuleric' is definitely one of mine) I see Ant and Dec walking out onto the stage. During my time watching the show that day, I'd seen the boys come out on stage a few times, often interacting with the warmup guy and the audience to kill a bit of time when there was a delay in filming. Either because something had gone wrong or props needed to be set on stage. So my first reaction was 'What's gone wrong?' I had a vision of being asked to perform the whole thing again because someone had forgotten to press record and then the audience would have to fake their reaction and the judges would have to pretend it was the first time they'd heard it. Nightmare. Instead, the boys walked right past me, down the steps and up to the judge's table while the audience was chanting 'Press the gold, press the gold' and as Nathan had foreseen, obediently that's exactly what they did. Gold confetti fell all around us, louder cheering, Nathan hugging me while we both jumped top and down. The opposite of a nightmare.

Again what was broadcast was only a fraction of the experience that happened on stage that night. Someone in the audience had naughtily recorded it on their phone and had kindly sent it to me on social media which was lovely to see. As I was the last act to perform that day, all the judges came up on stage and there was lots of hugging, back in the day when that was still acceptable. Emmah came up on stage too while one of the crew negotiated with Alfie, still curled up on the floor to come and join us as well. It was a very strange moment to be standing there in front of a live audience, having a conversation with Alesha Dixon about songwriting. Simon held his arms open to give Emmah a hug who ducked underneath to grab Alfie as he finally made it to the stage leaving Simon standing there looking a little nonplussed. Finally, we were ushered into the wings when I was meant to have a chat on camera with Ant and Dec. I knew that would never be used because after about ten minutes Dec put his hand on my arm and said:

"I'll stop you there Jon because you're not making any sense!"

I have no idea what I was saying and apparently neither did they. Then another small film crew asked us to join them in the foyer of the theatre so they could film us leaving, the problem being that it was now so late, the main doors of the theatre had been locked so we faked it and just got as far as putting our hands on the door. What happened next was so funny and mortifying at the same time and yet one of the reasons that I love my wife... One of the crew asked us if we could go back into the holding area at the hotel as they needed to film some shots with Emmah and the boys. I was ready to go and would have continued doing exactly what I had been told until well into the next day had Emmah not just said "Fuck off!" to a visibly shocked producer.

"We've been here since ten o'clock this morning and Jon has continually told you that we were staying at the hotel should you need to film us and now that he's got the golden buzzer you realise you haven't got enough footage. Well, I'm sorry, my youngest son is beyond exhausted so we are going back to our hotel room to celebrate and order champagne on room service!" Or something to that effect.

I might make her sound scarier than she is but to give the producer his due, he understood and we reached a compromise. As they were due to be filming at The Lowry in Salford the following week, we agreed that we'd meet them there and they could fake some footage as if it was at the Palladium. More hugs from some of the crew who had been nothing but delightful all day with a few even saying how happy they were that I'd got the golden buzzer as they were rooting for me, and we were back in the hotel room phoning my Mum plus a few others while drinking overpriced champagne in our overpriced hotel room. Showbiz baby.

Chapter 2
The First Semi-Final Song
February 2020

It was a tough secret to keep. We told a few family members and a couple of close friends but I wanted others to experience it when it was broadcast in April so we did manage to keep it pretty quiet. I now had the advantage of knowing that I needed to write something for the semi-finals which at the time were scheduled to be held as usual around June. I was inspired to write something the following week when coincidentally I was working with Jamie again on board a ship. We spent a lot of the week together celebrating the golden buzzer and I made sure to take him out to the poshest restaurant on board for a steak dinner to say thank you for his help. It was walking back from that dinner and its accompanying wine that I nearly fell down some stairs. Jamie is a strapping 6'4 so had no trouble reaching out and catching me with the immortal words:

"Jon, don't die. That would be a waste of the golden buzzer."

I've since told this story substituting my wife for Jamie (that's the only time I've done that) but the truth is it was Jamie who made me start laughing and then as we ordered the first round of Old Fashioneds, our favourite whiskey cocktail, we both somehow ended up singing along simultaneously to some chorus that I had invented that was keeping us giggling like school children… imagine some bouncy, cockney-type number with lots of knee bending and lyrics along the lines of:

I must not die! That would be a tragic waste for me
I must not die! Now I'm in the semis of BGT
I must not die, I must not die… oh, oh, oh, I must not die…

It continued in this improvised vein for a good thirty minutes as the Old Fashioned's flowed and we found it funnier and funnier. At the same time in my slightly fuzzy brain, I was thinking this song might have potential. The next morning after breakfast and a couple of Aspirin, I made my way to the piano bar which was empty as we were cruising down the Amazon River (no doubt Jeff Bezos owns that by now) and everyone was on the decks desperately trying to spot monkeys, crocodiles and those elusive piranha fish. Or at the very least the skeleton of a cow bobbing past the ship having been stripped of its flesh in thirty seconds by the piranhas as was the rumour. Probably started by the piranhas. What happened next I attribute to the inspirational properties of both my favourite whiskey cocktail and the company of Jamie, but I wrote almost a complete song which would remain mostly unchanged right up to the performance, in about thirty minutes.

As I was writing the song I was also imagining the production. It was still a jaunty, uptempo, knee-bending type composition in juxtaposition with its subject matter which was part of its appeal. But then I was also picturing a chorus line of showgirls in sequins and high heels at the end joining me in the chorus: "He must not die, (I must not die), He must not die, (I must not die)… as it led to a climax of orchestration and piano, ideally ending with me standing on top of the piano as it explodes.

I called Jamie in his cabin.

"I think I have something for the semi-finals."

"Excellent. I'm on my way."

Jamie agreed that it was definitely an original song and very funny. His argument was a valid one and an opinion that I wasn't used to, having been performing on the cruise ships for so many years and being very aware that the minority whom you could occasionally offend were the ones that wrote letters to head office. Jamie argued that people who liked it and found it funny would love it and others may not get it but that's OK. When you're broadcasting to millions, it doesn't hurt to try and find your niche. It would consequently help to sell tickets for my tour when the audience who love it and realise they share my sense of humour, rush out to buy tickets, regardless of whether I've even made it to the finals of the show. I even came up with a little trick that I wanted to play on Ant and Dec at the end of the song in the hope that it could create a 'viral' moment. After the piano collapses and I am revealed to still be alive, one of the boys hands me a microphone for my chat with the judges. I planned to hide a 'spark ring' in my hand. This is a magician's prop, widely available in all good joke shops, that winds up and when a button is pushed, it releases a wheel against a flint sending a stream of silver sparks out of your hand. When the performance is over and indeed I have not died, as they hand me the mic I would fake electrocution sending a shower of sparks out from the microphone while collapsing on the floor. The plan was not to tell Ant and Dec about any of it and simply record their reaction. I sent a rough recording of the song to the producers and got a reply that they loved it. While it was a little dark, it was funny and original and I should do it in the semi-finals. They were even up for pranking Ant and Dec. It was a weight off my mind knowing the stress of writing another song for the show had been dealt with. Remember this was early February and the world was just spinning around like it has done for a billion years or so while someone in China was eating a bat... (I think that was actually in December 2019 but why spoil a convenient timeline with accurate facts?)

Chapter 3
Because Of A Bat: Into Hell
March 2020

I remember first reading about some new virus in some faraway land, or more likely hearing it on the news. I try to avoid reading newspapers. I miss the days when they were best used for wrapping fish and chips. Some people were getting ill and it sounded horrible. It wouldn't affect me though, I was far too busy planning my mid-life career success. By early February, the UK had a few cases but they were all people who had been to the Far East. I was fine. Unusually, all of my recent cruise contracts had been closer to home. By Valentine's Day, the UK had nine cases. I still wasn't worried, although my Mum didn't send me a card that year like she had every year at my boy's boarding school so my friends would think I had a girlfriend. I of course used to immediately recognise my Mum's handwriting on the envelope and so began my love of acting as I would feign excitement at which one of the many girls clamouring for my attention had sent me a card declaring their love.

Less than a week later, the Diamond Princess cruise ship disembarked its passengers with six hundred and ninety-one people infected. There was talk of other cruise lines cancelling trips. By the end of February, the UK had twenty-three confirmed cases. On my Birthday, the 4th of March, Hong Kong reported the first confirmed case of a human giving the virus to a dog and the UK's infected had increased to eighty-four. I and all my fellow entertainers began receiving emails advising that ship contracts were being cancelled. There was a very real danger of Covid stealing my limelight and I wasn't impressed.

I won't go into more details and statistics here. If you want a detailed timeline, go check out Wikipedia like I did while writing this.

Suffice it to say that on Nathan's birthday, the 23rd of March, the UK went into lockdown and I had no work left in my diary for the foreseeable future.

Oh, and people were dying. Everywhere.

Speaking of diaries, I shall pepper this entertaining prose with a few extracts from the only diary I have ever kept. Weirdly, I began writing a diary on January 1st 2020. That's nothing unusual, I have started many diaries on the 1st of January, all of which have fizzled to nothing usually by January 7th but for some reason, I kept writing this one, long before my audition and certainly long before Corona was anything other than a beer. It's been a great resource while writing this book and will help to fill a few holes when I'm feeling too lazy to translate my barely legible writing into coherent paragraphs.

DIARY EXTRACT

Mar 23rd: Nathan's Birthday and lockdown. We've made the best of the situation. Nath is back into Lego but only Star Wars so that was expensive. Alf has started his home-schooling. Neither he nor his Mum or Dad is impressed. Boris on TV. Three-week minimum lockdown, no leaving home unless essential. This shit is real. Em feeling exhausted and bad headache.

Mar 24th: First full day of captivity. So I took the dogs out. Think that's allowed or they'd better send someone from the government to clean all the shit up. Our dogs refuse to poo within 500 yards of the house. Took a detour from my usual route over the fields and ended up in a bog. The dogs were chest-deep so had to pick them both up. Managed to stagger to a high wall with a road on the other side but couldn't get over it. A woman appeared on the other side and asked if she could help me. I asked if she could take the dogs so I could climb over but she said no, she wanted to know what I was doing on her land! I said I'd taken a wrong turn and she said don't do it again and walked away! Unbelievable. Had to call Em to drive out and rescue me.

Mar 25th: Newspaper article says BGT will be delayed but not the auditions. They're still due to be broadcast in April. If the semis are delayed it just means I get to be famous for a little bit longer. Did a shop at Asda and wore a mask for the first time. Quite busy but people keeping two metres apart and staff controlling people in and out. All cruise contracts are cancelled until at least May.

Mar 26th: Hosted an online quiz that finished at 7pm then we all gathered on doorsteps to clap the NHS at 8pm. Nathan appeared from his bedroom and joined in then as we were walking back into the house he admitted he thought everyone was clapping for my quiz! Pissed myself laughing.

Mar 27th: BGT press office called and asked if I could remove a tweet they'd found: "Simon Cowell is a dick. What does he know about cruise ships?" Posted back in 2009 when he was still using the cruises as a put-down for acts that he thought were a bit cheesy. Oops! Christ knows how many other social media faux pars are out there. Found out I won't be eligible for a self-employed grant as I have a limited company that I only started last year. Shit timing.

Mar 28th: Local shop's fruit and veg area looks like a swarm of locusts has decimated it. Just a few leaves left. Remarkable. BGT has said I may be on This Morning with Phil and Holly, could I think about writing a song? Still not allowed to announce that I'm on the show and may only find out on the Thursday before I'm due to be broadcast on Saturday.

April 18th: My audition was broadcast. Quite emotional seeing Nath and Alfie's reactions even though a lot of the shots of Alfie looking emotional were actually because he was knackered! But secretly glad they don't let the truth get in the way of a good story. They also cut a couple of lines of the song. Not sure why. They were funny lines and they messed up the rhyming scheme but hey ho. Not sure they'll be able to use any of the home video recordings that they asked us to do while we watched the broadcast. After the first cut, Emmah and I looked at each other a bit perplexed but after the second one Emmah announced "What the fuck?!" They should have expected it after her last outburst at the Palladium. We had friends and family on a group Zoom during the broadcast and I was glad we hadn't told everyone about the buzzer. It was quite emotional watching all their reactions.

April 19th: The day after the night before! Crazy on social media. My YouTube video is trending at #2 with 800k views. Got the most amazing message from a school friend whom I haven't spoken to in over 20 years. Made me cry.

I'll print some of the message here. Only because it sums up a lot of my childhood at boarding school in quite a succinct way. It also makes me sound like a lovely person:

> Hi Jon. Many congratulations - it was amazing. I've been meaning to write for a while with the following but I always managed to forget. Seeing you last night (and the re-watches my boys insisted on today) has been a great and timely reminder.
> Our two boys are now 12 and 14, after initially learning the piano they started to lose interest and began to question why they were doing it so one evening at dinner I told them about my friend at school. He wasn't a cool kid; he didn't play rugby and didn't throw his weight around. He was sometimes picked on but was never mean to anyone. This had my boy's attention as it resonated with them. I explained that my friend wasn't amazing at sport but he could sing, play the piano and

do some pretty impressive magic tricks. I told them that when we went to our local pub, my friend could go in there amongst the boys showing off for the local girls, sit down at the piano and grab the attention of everyone with his playing. He didn't need to be coarse to be cool, he had something far more appealing: a talent.

I also explained that one year he and his parents invited me to stay with them after they'd moved to Cyprus. I didn't have much money for drinks but to my surprise that didn't matter. We would go into a bar and this friend would sit at the piano and smash out some tunes. His payment? Drinks for him and his friend.

Something changed in my sons after that story. They began to play more regularly and instead of grades, they just pursued playing pieces that they enjoyed. Neither are brilliant pianists but they understand that they now have an amazing gift, one that can bring people together, inspire them and create joy. Before last night they would sometimes ask me to recount the story of my friend, Jon. Seeing you on TV and the reaction you received last night just hammered home the power of talent and hard work. It was incredible to watch and I know the boys will remember it for a long time to come.

You'll touch the lives of many more people in your journey and you won't know you've done it or the influence you've had. So this story is a reminder that even small moments can affect people's lives, and are to be cherished just as much as the big ones.

All the best best, we'll be watching your progress with wonder. Tim

It's only occurred to me reading that again now that Tim may have planted the seed for the song I wrote for the Finals show in that last paragraph. Weird how things burrow into your brain and can sit there until they're needed. I may owe Tim a beer or two. On the same subject, I found a video recently of Alfie when he was very young making up one of his songs. I had been working away for a couple of weeks and was due home the next day. His little face as he looked into his Mum's iPhone singing the heart-wrenching (if a little repetitive) words:

"My Daddy is coming home. I'm so happy.

My Daddy is coming home. Yay.

My Daddy is coming home. He's not just Daddy on the phone.

My Daddy is coming home. Yay."

Emmah had to remind me of this loving lyric months after my audition and months after I had written:

"And his children ask 'Daddy, when are you coming home?'

This game is not the same when you're just 'Daddy on the phone'."

It's usually difficult to explain where inspiration springs from so it's quite lovely when you can find a source and quite bewildering when you discover it was not a conscious decision to use it.

In juxtaposition to Tim's inspiring note, there were also one or two nutters in the social media-verse and the press team on the show had warns all the contestants that this could be the case. Their recommendation to not read any on-line comments must be regularly ignored by any self-respecting performer who is willing to acknowledge that they are a delicate wallflower with bookish sensibilities and fragile egos who will risk accidentally reading the wrath of trolls to find any self-affirming comments written by fans. I was quite impressed that I didn't find more vitriol than I did, but there was enough for me to feel inspired to write a song on April 18th, according to my diary, called Baldy With A Buzzer utilising some of the online abuse. (The lyrics are part of the appendix in this book if you want to giggle at some of the creative insults that I found written about me.)

Let me give you some advice: don't ever decide to create anything that requires you to Google yourself repeatedly looking for criticism. It's not a fun way to spend an afternoon. In this case, however, it was quite therapeutic and a good enough song in my opinion for it to become a staple part of my stage show to this day. With the comments flashing up on the screen behind me, I somehow took away the power of these faceless vermin and instead got theatres full of people laughing at them. I only wish I'd kept their real profile names and photos in the show but I was warned that it could have led to some legal entanglements.

Chapter 4
Lockdown
April-May 2020

Now I have to tell you at this point that we ROCKED lockdown. Yes, we had something huge to look forward to but also we were about to begin friendships with local families that haven't existed between neighbours since the war. Allegedly.

We live in a small cul-de-sac (that's French. The word, not our cul-de-sac. That's English. In a small village near Manchester called Mossley to be precise. I do like the derivation of words and phrases though. Cul de sac actually translates as 'bottom of the bag' and even the French don't use it to mean a dead-end like we do. They say 'voie sans issue'. I realise too late that this tangent is really too long for parentheses and I should have used a footnote. I'll try to remember that going forward) of only seven houses that were built in 2017. We all moved in at the same time and had been friendly enough up until now to say good morning or even offer to put someone else's bins out. Not to do it without asking obviously but to offer. Baby steps.

While we were the oldest residents in our 40s, everyone was certainly part of the same generation with a couple of kids born around the same time too. We were about to advance to the automatic-bin-moving stage very rapidly. I honestly can't remember how our first evening fire-pit began but somehow a few of us ended up sitting around one in the middle of our English cul de sac, all socially distanced, enjoying beer, wine and convivial chat. It was very pleasant and we agreed to do it the next night, and the next. Then on the third night, a game-changer… I wheeled our tennis table out from our back garden where it had sat since Christmas after I bought it as a family present, covered it with a tarpaulin and then let it become a large, flat, ugly garden ornament. Turns out every guy on our [...] was equally good (bad?) at ping-pong. A game that can safely be played two metres apart. I can only assume that neighbours in the war had fire pits, perhaps natural ones from German bombs, plus some communal, low-impact sport that led to the kind of friendships that I had only heard about from my Grandparents because it certainly worked for us. However sexist it may sound, the ladies sat gossiping, drinking Prosecco while the men played sports and occasionally poked the fire while drinking beer. (I may have also made some excellent Pornstar Martinis just to keep the testosterone level down.) If it hadn't been for the raging death toll and the pandemic ravaging the world, it would have been idyllic.

By the end of the first week of lockdown, we had become firm friends oiled with flowing booze and waking up regularly smelling like Guy Fawkes. My Wife put a slight damper on my laid-back life when she pointed out that with the world suffering through a pandemic, did I think I should still go on national television and sing a song called I Must Not Die? I pointed out that I wrote it at least four weeks before Corona and she pointed out that she knew that but the public may not. It might appear in poor taste. I didn't agree. This was one of the funniest songs I had ever written. A producer on the show also loved it and recommended I perform it on the show. Emmah pointed out that they probably hadn't heard of Corona either when they showed such enthusiasm. I sulked off and video-called my good friend Phil Butler to play him the song. He pointed out that Emmah was right and I immediately agreed with him and Emmah face palmed herself. I was going to need a new song.

I want to digress slightly here with a footnote that is too long to even be a footnote. On my tour in 2021, we were setting up and doing the tech at the Hazlitt Theatre in Maidstone on the 18th of October when Jamie Allan called me and asked if I'd heard the terrible news. I hadn't. The night before our mutual friend Phil Butler had been found dead in his cabin on the P&O ship where he was performing his comedy show. He was 51 years old.

We'd met when I was sixteen and he was eighteen at a magic convention in Suffolk. Two fresh-faced youths with full heads of hair. We lost touch a couple of years later until 2015 when I was at Pete Matthews home, to participate in a charity show. I felt a tap on my shoulder and was greeted by the dazzling bald head above the even more dazzling smile of Phil. It turns out that he was also the closest of friends with Pete but his name had never come up when Pete and I had been chatting. All very strange. Neither of us knew that we were mates with Phil. It was a lovely reunion and we stayed in touch after that, all the time including a fabulous few days in an AirBnB for a boy's weekend with Pete, Jamie and another great friend Neal Austin. It would be the last time that we would see Phil.

The news of his sudden death hit me quite hard and I had to leave the theatre to find a quiet space. I called Emmah and I called my Mum telling them that I loved them and I messaged Pete knowing how his heart would be broken and telling him that I was there to chat when he felt that he could. On stage that night Dr Showbiz took over and the show went on to a lovely, appreciative audience. I had no plans to mention Phil, not even certain that I could without an ensuing lump in my throat making it impossible to sing. Until I got to I Must Not Die. I found myself telling the audience about my phone call to Phil and dedicated the song to him, beginning to sing despite the lump in my throat and the tears in my eyes. I was worried that I'd made the moment too sentimental but after the show, Andy my tour manager assured me that I'd pitched it perfectly and that he was in bits and he'd never even met Phil. I'd like to think that Phil would have appreciated the irony of the song in the circumstances.

I do love a good bit of serendipity as well as the word itself, and a few days later Andy and I were due to be travelling past Heathrow still on my theatre tour when coincidentally Pete phoned and told me he was at an airport hotel before flying to join a cruise the next day. Our next show wasn't until a day later so we cancelled our plans for that evening and diverted to Pete's hotel where Andy and I booked rooms so we could all drink beer together and tell tales of Phil. It was an understandably emotional night made slightly surreal when in the quiet hotel bar, the only other customer at a table a few feet away started chatting with us:

"I couldn't help overhearing you all talking about Phil Butler. I knew him too."

It turns out that this chap was one of Phil's neighbours at Spielplatz, the UK's longest-running naturist resort where Phil had lived for many years. Phil wasn't a naturist until the opportunity came up to buy a property there for a very good price and he decided it was worth getting his tackle out for. On the day he moved in a television crew happened to be there filming a documentary and like so many of us were drawn to Phil and his megawatt smile. The presenter of the program asked if she could interview Phil which led to the fabulous exchange:

Presenter: We're here with one of Spielplatz' residents, Phil Butler. Hello Phil. How long have you been a naturist for?

Phil: (Looking at his watch) Um… about two and a half hours!

There are so many Phil stories that I could tell you here but this is enough for now. I still miss him every day but he left a fabulous legacy of laughter and great stories with us who knew him as well as anyone lucky enough to see him on stage.

After Phil's advice and his confirmation of the validity of my Wife's advice, I needed to come up with a plan B for the semi-finals. I had written a song around the time of the millennium about my Mum and Dad that had become a regular part of my stage show ever since. It was called When I Was A Boy and I had made a slideshow to accompany it which played on the big screens behind me during the song. Mum had been a star in the Ipswich Operatic Dramatic Society since she was a teenager, often taking the lead roles in their productions. She was a fantastic performer with a great voice and a good actor too. Not that I'm biased but she was very good. There might have been an opportunity for her to go to RADA and pursue it professionally but we won't mention that. Instead, she met my Dad when she was twenty-four and Dad was a little older, by eighteen years. Being the swinging 70s, Mum wasted no time asking Dad out on a date which led to marriage and me.

Dad was also a fantastic performer and his knowledge of stagecraft was to be invaluable to me as I pursued my career. He could spin a great yarn too, (I think 'raconteur' is the word if we're compiling French vocabulary. Interestingly, a female raconteur is a raconteuse.) He could sell a song as well. His rendition with my Mum of 'Honeysuckle And The Bee' was the highlight of many dinner parties and family gatherings. I've just recently found a video of Mum and Dad singing Shadow of Your Smile together at a karaoke evening in Cyprus where we lived when I was 18. Dad removes his glasses to look romantically into my Mum's eyes while purposefully and short-sightedly walking into the mic stand. Very funny. Made all the better by the guy running the karaoke completely missing the joke and picking up the mic stand while glaring at Dad.

Dad helped me with many aspects of stagecraft that are so important to learn, like how to take a bow and leave a stage and the importance of timing and articulation. I had a habit of pronouncing my R's as W's as a child and Dad said that would never work on stage. Luckily he didn't give the same advice to Jonathan Ross. Or maybe unluckily, perhaps it would have kept him off our screens all these years. (The only person who was rude to me at the after-show party at the National Television Awards. Apparently I haven't got over it yet.)

Dad was also quite an accomplished pianist and he taught me how to play chords when I was very young so I could read simple chord charts with vocal lines. I picked it up rather quickly and was soon helping Mum learn new songs for her performances with Barrington's Old Time Music Hall. 'My Old Man Said Follow The Van', 'Why Am I Always The Bridesmaid?' and that timeless classic 'Ta Ra Ra Boomdeay'. All of which I can still remember today despite having not played them since I was about ten years old. It was like learning a second language and children can do that so quickly that it becomes second nature. That's my only explanation for my ability to learn to play by ear so efficiently.

I used to come home from my Primary School where we would sing a hymn every morning and be able to play the hymn when I got home. Tunes I heard on the radio or television came quickly to me at the piano and when Mum and I both began trying to learn 'Home On The Range' from an old 'Teach-Yourself-Piano' record, I was playing it after just one listen. During this time, Dad just stopped playing the piano. I never asked him about it, he just stopped. Of course, he never stopped teaching me. When I had my first digital piano in my bedroom I would work my way through one of the early 'fake' books which had just vocal lines and chord symbols, perfect for my style of improvising, and every wrong note or chord would be met with a yell from the living room: "NO!" Or a loud sucking of teeth. Often I would yell back: "I KNOW! I'M STILL LEARNING IT!!" In this way, I soon had a huge repertoire of songs going right back to the 1920s, perfect for my upcoming tour of retirement homes when I was twelve years old.

I found a publicity leaflet recently that Dad had printed for me in his office as Hall-keeper of Suffolk County Council. The last line of my bio, already quite short as I'd only had twelve years to try and accomplish anything at this point, had the immortal line: 'What he lacks in professionalism, he more than makes up for with enthusiasm.' Followed by: 'No fee is necessary but Jonathan would appreciate a donation to your local RSPCA.' Luckily Dad was a better teacher than a manager or financial advisor.

The truth is, at this point, I had no real desire to pursue a career with a piano. Because I'd been playing it since I was four years old, it didn't feel like much of a skill or talent. Instead, I was quite obsessed with magic tricks. Tommy Cooper was a household name at the time, the bumbling 6'4" clown with size thirteen shoes whose magic tricks famously failed as he coughed and blundered his way through hilarious routines with all the familiar props that Paul Daniels was simultaneously using to great effect on his television show. Mum and Dad bought me a magic set when I was around seven years old and I spent hours learning sleight of hand with coins and cards. The perfect hobby for an only child who had regular, captive audiences at my parents' dinner parties (this was the early 80's and dinner parties were very popular). I would beg my Dad to let me show everyone my latest trick and he would reluctantly say "Just one!" It was a huge deal a few years later with my skills a bit more polished when Dad called me from my bedroom: "Jonathan, come and show everyone that new card trick you've learnt". I was beaming from ear to ear. Perhaps my professionalism was getting closer to my enthusiasm.

I'm in danger of dwelling too much on those 'boring' early years before I've even touched on the celebrity gossip of more recent times so I'll leave this here suffice to say that both Mum and Dad were a huge influence on my career choices growing up so it was easy to write a song in tribute to them. It was a simple, nostalgic look back at those early years but was a big hit in my stage show with people telling me afterwards that they were moved to tears. I thought perhaps with a little thought and revamp it could be brought up to date for the semi-final show. I could add a few verses to acknowledge the hell that the world was experiencing plus a few more light-hearted moments to remind people that my first career choice was to make people laugh rather than cry.

At this point, no one knew if the semi-finals were still going to go ahead. I remember Amanda Holden saying in some interview that under no circumstances would they consider doing the show without a live theatre audience but that was looking less likely as the lockdown was extended with no real end in sight. There was even talk of the show being delayed until the following year but at least no one was considering cancelling it completely. Imagine that as a tragic twist of fate after being teased with a golden buzzer. It did mean that I had months to second guess my choice of song and to keep re-writing it. Around this time I had a phone call with one of the producers who asked if I'd like to have a session with one of their hired writers on the show, Steve Dunne.

"We offer his services to all our comedy acts... would you like to chat with him as well?"

As well?! I was sensing that I had already been pigeonholed as 'the middle-aged piano guy that tells Dad jokes' but I accepted their offer and an appointment was set up for Steve and me to meet at the ITV studios for a writing session. I was quite nervous about collaborating with someone I'd never met but I needn't have worried. Steve and I hit it off and within a few hours we'd polished what I'd already written and the final version was sent to Beth.

Beth is the creative director of the show and she comes up with some crazy ideas for the stage sets for the performances. Whether it's actual fire or pyrotechnics, billowing silk sheets covering the stage or people flying in on wires, it seems that no idea or budget is out of the question. I was excited to see what ideas she had for my song.

"Jon, I've got big plans for your semi-final performance…"

"Ooo… I'm very excited"

"We're going to keep it simple."

"Oh'"

"A white grand piano centre stage and we'll project old photos of your parents onto the lid of the piano as you're singing. It will look beautiful."

"No fire or pyros?"

"Um… no."

"Can I fly in on a wire?"

"Why?"

"Because it would still be cheaper than what I originally wanted to do in the semi-finals."

We'll get to that in a bit. Beth also asked if I felt I could write a song to use in my semi-final VT (that's technical speak for a video track, any film footage that is used during a performance). In the past, a couple of other keyboard acts on the show had both written an original song that BGT filmed a music video around and it was shown before their semi-final performances. I didn't want to be pigeonholed as 'another BGT keyboard act' so resisted but it was pointed out to me that this was another opportunity for the viewers to see my talent without taking up any stage time. Most acts were simply interviewed and could all be heard saying familiar soundbites like "It would mean the world to me…", "It would be a dream come true…", "I love the Queen and to perform for her would be an honour…", or "Simon Cowell's a dick. What does he know about cruise ships?"

Maybe their idea to not interview me was the right one. They stipulated that it could be no longer than one minute so my first idea was The One Minute Song. While creative people often can't explain where inspiration comes from, I can acknowledge this was heavily influenced by a Tim Minchin song that he'd performed on the Royal Variety Show in 2007 called The Three Minute Song. Only in as much that I had to sing a song in one minute whereas he had three times as long.

I love Tim and I think he is a genius. Both lyrically and musically. Some of the greatest accolades I've ever had are when people compliment me in the same sentence as Tim, Victoria Wood, Bill Bailey, Dudley Moore, or Victor Borge. My point is that we're all standing on the shoulders of giants. Whatever your job you may well be compared to others who do a similar thing, hopefully in a positive light but there will always be the comments: "He's not as good as...." Or "He's copying...." I like to think there's room for us all. I do make an effort to not be influenced too much by people in this business who are funny, play the piano, or sing, but I also get inspired by them. It's a thin line.

I was quite happy with my one-minute song and even made a video to go along with it where I was going about my usual daily routines, making coffee, having cereal, getting dressed etc. as gold confetti kept falling out of various spaces around the house. It poured out of the kettle, shot out of the toaster, fell out of the fridge and was jammed in the arm of my coat. I ignored it every time as if it happened every day and just continued singing my song. But it turns out it didn't fit the brief, not that I knew there was a brief. It seems I *was* being 'sold' as the piano man who told Dad jokes, a loving family guy, and they wanted more of that in the song. What I'd written was a little too frivolous. What they wanted was more cheese. Not cowbell. So I came up with a full-on cheese-fest of a song called 'Long Time Coming' and wrote it pretty quickly. They loved it but the problem at the moment was that they weren't allowed to send a film crew out to make the video to go with it. Having seen the video I'd made for the One Minute Song they asked if I'd be up for filming the footage myself and they would edit it. Not the high-profile television experience I was hoping for, instead it was just me, with a tripod gaffer taped into the back of my car filming myself driving 'to a gig'. I also spoke to Dermott, the owner of our local bar The Gillery, to ask if I could film a fake 'show' there to use in the film. He agreed with the condition that I'd do a show in his bar for real when it was allowed to reopen.

Two weeks later we got the news that they had permission to use a film crew after all so my amateur footage never saw an editing suite. I just rewatched some of it and it's probably just as well. So a small crew arrived at our home and it was a fun day's filming at our friend's house doubling as ours as they had a lovely vintage upright piano which matched the look we were going for rather than my digital model with wires and microphones attached. We did some shots in our home of the kids and some fake 'We're leaving for the theatre' moments with us shouting upstairs to the boys and then all of us getting in the car and driving off. Truly buttock-clenching awful VT that thank god was never used. You can see similar moments in many of the VT segments for other contestants.

Then we'd arranged for family and friends to join us at The Gillery and that was six hours of filming for what was less than six seconds on film! Crazy. Our neighbours joined us and one of them, Joe, with his skinhead and tattooed arms, was chosen as a suitably scary-looking member of the audience to throw a drink in my face. A rare moment of light-heartedness that I was insisting they use, in the otherwise quite emotional song. It only took about four takes as I got more and more soaked. Luckily my head was quick to dry off for the next take while water was still dripping down my back to my arse. More showbiz baby. The remaining footage would be filmed at the studios in September. You can see the finished video on YouTube on my channel. www.youtube.com/@JonCourtenay

Chapter 5
Live Television

At the beginning of lockdown, I was spending a lot of time at my digital piano in our lounge and when my audition was broadcast I often had to lock the family out while I did a virtual interview, often live on prime-time TV. This Morning got in touch and asked if I'd be up for a Zoom call and if I'd be prepared to perform an original song on the show. These song requests were going to become a familiar part of my life, often very last minute and very daunting to a guy who has never thought of himself as a songwriter. I always used music as a prop for my comedy but since my audition was broadcast, I was the guy that could write feel-good songs that could transport a listener from fits of laughter to tears of emotion and pathos. It was a very sudden career change and often quite a bit of pressure.

Of course, I told the ITV producer that I would be happy to perform a song on the show even if it would have to be from the comfort of my lounge. My mind started racing. I'd already bought a large green screen and lighting and commandeered one end of our lounge as my small but functional studio. I Googled 'This Morning sofa' and found an up-to-date photo of the studio which I then transferred to my green screen, even managing to prop one of our cushions that Emmah had bought me with a photo of a golden buzzer on it, on a box hidden behind the green screen but at the perfect height so that it looked as if it was on the sofa in the studio. My idea was to magically grab the cushion from their sofa at some point to get a reaction from the hosts Phillip Schofield and Holly Willoughby.

As far as the song was concerned, I had come up with an idea lamenting the fact that I couldn't be with them in the studio so had gone to all this trouble. Yes, I could see and hear them but I couldn't smell them and I had it on good albeit fictional authority that Holly had a lovely scent about her. As I type this I realise it does sound a little stalker-ish and Twitter wasn't slow to agree with me. I thought it was funny though, and more importantly, so did Emmah so the Twitter-twits could do one.

Holly's Song

Always hoped my big break on British TV
Would get me on This Morning with Phil and Holly,
But then this damn virus came and spoilt everything,
So instead of on your sofa, I'm just video-calling.

I've spoken to people who have been on the show,
Who actually made it to the studio,
And all of them told me without hesitation
That Holly is a wonderful scent sensation.

So Holly I'm sorry I can't tell you
How upset I might get now I can't smell you.

Maybe it's just whatever perfume you wear,
Or your underarm spray of the stuff in your hair,
Whatever the reason you sweeten the air,
And that's why I'm gutted I can't physically be there.

Now we all know the world is a happier place
Because every morning on This Morning we see your face,
But I know we'd be happier if we all got a whiff,
So we need a TV with scratch and sniff.

Now Holly it's clearly a personal view
Of everyone I've spoken to who has met you,
And Phillip I'm sure that you smell good too,
But there are times, like Christmas when only Holly will do.

So Holly this may be just wild speculation,
But I think you could help the entire population,
Just bottle your smell and sell the inhalation,
And then it won't seem too bad in self-isolation.

I had everything set up and was ready to go in plenty of time for the call from the producers ten minutes before I was due to be broadcast. They had called the day before to make sure that everything was working and had insisted that I use Skype instead of the Zoom app that was rapidly growing in popularity. It took some tweaking to get the green screen working with Skype but I'd sussed it and was rearing to go. The call came through on time:

"Hi Jon. This Morning producer here. How are you?"

"Great thanks. Excited to be on the show."

"Brilliant! Love your studio's green screen. You've gone to a lot of trouble."

"It's no problem. Got to make the most of the video call opportunities... Hello?... You still there?"

[Long pause]

"Jon, we seem to be having a problem with your connection."

"Oh. Well, I've switched off every other device in the house as you asked me to. Much to the annoyance of both my sons who are now X-Box-less..."

It's now only five minutes until I'm due on the show.

"We'll try and tweak it at our end, Jon. Stand by..."

Two more minutes…

"Jon, do you have Zoom?"

I don't even have time to facepalm myself as I yank out cables and plug new ones in, frantically trying to set it all up in the sixty seconds I have left. I click on the link that they frantically emailed to me and then I can see myself on my monitor, the studio photo still there on the green screen as they count me down from twenty seconds and I realise my golden buzzer cushion is now floating a few inches above the floor and very obviously NOT on the sofa as the aspect ratio settings of Zoom are just different enough from Skype to make it levitate. No time, Phil is already introducing me. I decide to grab the cushion right at the top of the show giving everyone less chance to notice my impressive, impromptu magic trick. The hosts seem suitably impressed but I know I rushed it and I'm already sweating.

The chat goes well and then they ask about an original song that they've been told I've written for them. I'd had to send it to the producers so they could make sure it wasn't offensive or too weird but Phil and Holly had no idea what was coming. You can tell if you watch it back and focus on Phil's face. He gradually becomes more and more uncomfortable as I sing about my strange obsession with Holly's smell. The scratch-and-sniff TV line contorts his face into a slightly incredulous awkwardness instead of the guffaw that I had hoped for. Holly is loving it though and laughing in all the right places. The end of the song is greeted by Phil's comment:

"Well, that was all levels of bizarre!"

Followed by his explanation that if I was there in the studio I would be very disappointed as since they'd had no guests on the show during lockdown, Holly had let herself go and was pretty stinky these days. I laughed slightly nervously at Phil's joke and wondered how much more awkward the interview could go. I needn't have worried. My Wife was on hand to make sure that the song about smells would not be what I remembered most from that day. As the interview was wrapping up, Alfie appeared in the doorway waving and then jumped behind the piano into the shot. That was quite cute I suppose so Phil and Holly duly acknowledged him and waved. What they weren't expecting was Emmah to follow him and peer over my shoulder frantically waving. They'd been watching it live in the bedroom and saw their chance to be on TV before the interview ended. I was mortified. To this day Emmah doesn't agree that she did anything wrong. Despite many friends and family pausing the program to grab a screenshot and superimpose her into all kinds of famous situations; the Mona Lisa, the Last Supper and many more, she's very proud of her appearance on daytime TV.

I was going to need a studio with a lock on the door.

The whole clip is available on my YouTube channel.

Chapter 6
The Studio
August 2020

We had an integral garage attached to the house that had never seen a car since we lived there. Instead, like most people's garages these days, it had become storage for boxes of crap most of which hadn't been opened in more than a year. I suggested to Emmah that we could convert it into a studio and spare bedroom and that I could do most of the work myself as I was currently quite unemployed so it would save us thousands of pounds. I'd done the same on our previous home and there isn't a lot you can't find on YouTube if you get stuck. I'd need an electrician to advise me on adding sockets and lights and a bricklayer would need to be employed to fill the void where the garage door was and to install the window, but I could raise the floor and insulate the walls myself. I also decided to build a stud wall at one end making a utility room accessed from the kitchen so I'd need to knock through to make the doorway. YouTube said it was pretty straightforward so I began planning.

I'm very happy with graph paper, a ruler and a quality retracting pencil. My favourite place at school was the woodworking shop where I spent most of my free time building and creating, and back then I had to learn from a real carpenter, in the flesh. YouTube was a long way away. Mr. Hall was the CDT teacher and he was a lovely guy, inspiring me to learn how to make dovetails, mortice and tenon joints and to try and draw a thirty-degree angle freehand for an isometric diagram. (That was his party piece. I said he was lovely, not the life and soul of a social gathering). So I had a basic knowledge of DIY and I could borrow a jackhammer to break through the kitchen wall so I figured I was ready.

To find a bricklayer I used the modern Yellow Pages… (Google it if you're too young. Generations will never know the catchphrase 'Let your fingers do the walking') and posted it on Facebook. I got a recommendation from a girl I'd never met but who was very local and said her boyfriend was a fabulous bricklayer and very reasonable. I sent him a message and he agreed to come and take a look. The first warning sign was when only one of his eyes was looking at me. I kid you not. I've met a few people with lazy eyes over the years and always find it very uncomfortable only looking at their good eye when they're speaking to me. I'm sure you've been in a similar situation so if you take nothing else from this book, let me alleviate your potential future anxiety and give you a tip: if you look at the space between someone's eyes when they are talking to you, they have no idea that you're not looking them in the eye. Shall I repeat that? Or you can just read it again. And then try it. Right now, go and speak to the first person you can find and explain what I've said then try it. Although you may feel very strange staring at the skin between their eyes, they will not be able to tell that you're not intently looking into their soul via their pupils. It's not something you'd want to start doing in every conversation but when confronted with a lazy eye, or even worse, cross-eyes, this is the way to go. It also helps kill time if someone is boring the pants off you. You're welcome.

Despite the lazy eye, Dave the Brickie seemed to know what he was talking about and gave me a decent quote so I agreed that he could do the job and he agreed that he'd start the next day. Another warning sign; I'd been told that there was more work than brickies available so why could he start so quickly? All this is very easy to look back on in hindsight and also while reading my diary which rather than try to cover the next couple of weeks in descriptive and entertaining prose, I shall reprint here:

DIARY EXTRACT

Aug 3rd: Woke in a bad mood, don't know why. Lockdown blues maybe? Couldn't shake it all day. Worked on the semi-final song and ideas for a finals song if I make it. Did some of the singing exercises that Anni gave me. Decided to put a shed in the back garden to store some of the crap that I'm going to have to clear out of the garage.

Aug 5th: Teddy [one of our dogs] had shit all over the kitchen and hall during the night. [He *is* a shi-tzu] Cleared it up just in time for my interview on Zoom with Sun TV mag. Ooo the glamour. Mum phoned. Roxy [her dog] had the shits all over the lounge. She said she'd tried to clean it up but she's not good on her legs so I'm going over later with the carpet cleaner. Started clearing out the garage. Seriously running low on cash and Emmah wants to book a holiday!

Aug 6th: Booked a holiday for Emmah and Alfie in Turkey with Row [her Sister]. Great night around the fire pit with the neighbours. I was on ping-pong form and kicked some arse.

Aug 10th: Rewrote the song that I may use in the Finals. I wake up during the night and write notes on my phone. Feels very creative if a little knackering. Picking up the new shed tomorrow. The skin clinic phoned and they have referred me to have my mole removed ASAP. That can't be good.

Aug 11th: Picked up the shed in a hire van and built it the same day, on my own! Feel wrecked now but like any man, excited to have an empty shed to fill with my man-shit.

Aug 13th: It's the fourth day of a heatwave so I took Alfie to Blackpool. Moved the last of the loan money to our current account. That's it now. £5,000 left and we're skint and I've still got to find the money for the garage conversion. I've been quoted between £3-5,000 for a builder to do all the work. I reckon I can do it for less than £1,000. Necessity is the mother of self-build. Changed the words to my semi-final song after hearing about Simon's bike accident.

Aug 15th: I've been told I can't bring any family to the semi-finals recording due to Covid. That's going to suck.

Aug 17th: Took Em and Alf to the airport for their 2 weeks holiday in Turkey. Nath and I took dogs over the fields. Had to cut through a bit of a rough estate and a group of teens were loitering on a corner. Nath felt very anxious. Told him to just keep his head down. Just got past them and they shouted "Oi!" Then I started to feel anxious too.

"Ain't you the BGT bloke?"

"Yeah"

(To his mate) "See? Told ya. Can we have a photo please? You were fab. Up the Mossley!"

Aug 22nd: Finished clearing the garage and built the stud wall for the utility room. Doing electrics tomorrow then plaster-boarding. Want it all finished by the time Em gets back. Cunard has cancelled all cruises until March 2021!!

Aug 27th: Trip to London for backstage filming for semi-finals. The studio is HUGE! Got to hang out with Ant and Dec a bit while they were rehearsing their opening number. Hospital phoned. They've had a cancellation. I can have the mole removed tomorrow at 10am.

Aug 28th: The mole is gone! Yay. Painful injections for the anaesthetic but no pain after, obviously. The sound was pretty gross though so close to my ear. I could hear my flesh being sliced. Freaky. I filmed Mum's little bit for BGT this evening when they are going to show her on-screen at the end of my song. Hope it's not too cheesy.

Sept 1st: Train to London to record the semi-finals!!!

CHAPTER 7
The Semi-Finals
Sept 2020

As the name implies, I wanted to show Britain my talents so I was very keen to try and work some magic into my performance. Another late-night session with Jamie over a few more Old Fashioned's and I had the perfect combination of music, magic and the piano. I would write a song called 'Up In The Air' about how my life had been so crazy since my audition was broadcast and then just when I thought it was only my life that was up in the air, the piano would start to rise from the stage, with no visible means of support, and I would rise with it, still playing and singing. It would float across the stage and then miraculously begin to slowly turn 360 degrees along with me and the piano stool turning upside down simultaneously. It would gently return to the stage in time for the end of the song and incredulous applause barely covering the gasps of amazement. Sorted.

It was so good that I couldn't decide if it should be my final performance instead of the semis. But then if I didn't get through, I'd never get to do it. This is the paradox: do you perform your best material in the semi-finals to give you the best chance of getting through to the finals or do you hold something back and hope you still make it but then have a better chance of actually winning the whole show with your A-list material. It was keeping me awake at night. I decided to run it past Beth who made the choice very simple for me. Without wanting to incur the wrath of magicians all over the world, I'll paraphrase what Beth said:

"I know the magic illusion you're referring to and I know who manufactures it. Apart from it costing over £25,000 just to RENT for one performance, unfortunately with the venue that we're having to use for the show there just isn't the space available backstage to make it work."

So that was that. If you'd like to see a great version of the illusion, go to your favourite video-sharing website and check out 'Jinag Hao floating piano'. Don't get stuck down the rabbit hole and see David Nixon doing a version with Anita Harris, that cardboard instrument isn't fooling anyone. While I was disappointed at the time, it was serendipitous as I ended up in the final show with five magic acts! I was the last act on and no matter how impressive a floating piano or the other performers may have been, I think people were over the magic by the time I came on and if I suddenly started levitating, it would have made it less of a variety show and more like the Blackpool Magic Convention. But I'm getting ahead of myself again. Apologies if you're reading this with no idea who I am and now I've spoilt the surprise of me making it to the finals show. I should have typed 'SPOILER ALERT' and you could have chosen to skip it. However, if you bought this book for the suspense then you're probably already slightly disappointed and wishing you'd gone for the latest Peter James novel instead.

The other good thing that came from the original floating piano idea was the song. With a few tweaks and another session with Steve Dunne plus some subconscious memory of a letter from a school friend, it became 'Small Things' ('SPOILER ALERT') the song I performed in the finals. But we're not there yet, it's still the semi-finals and I have a song to sing.

It had been decided that the show would go ahead despite Covid. That would mean no live audience and also, no Simon Cowell. In August 2020 Simon fell off his electric bike damaging his spine and was out of action so Ashley Banjo, the creator of the dance group Diversity, who won the show in 2009 (the year that Susan Boyle came second) stepped in as a judge. It meant that instead of the

Hammersmith Apollo where the live shows are usually performed, we were at the LH2 studios in Acton, north London. A cavernous, warehouse of a studio where they have recorded The Voice and X-Factor in the past.

A virtual wall had been built surrounding the performance area at a huge expense (a lot more than a floating piano) so we could see all the people watching at home. It was very weird. I've been performing in front of live audiences since I was a kid and there is an energy in a theatre for a live show that you just can't replicate. Plus we had no audio in the studio. It would have been impossible to manage the audio input from a thousand individual streaming screens so it was all added after the show had been recorded which meant the only audience we could hear in the studio were the four judges. Or if you were really good, then a reaction from a cameraman or two but generally they'd heard and seen it all before. I'm glad the show could still go ahead but I missed a theatre audience and the atmosphere that it provided.

The other very strange experience was using in-ear monitors for the first time. I've always used 'live' monitors next to the piano, a speaker in which I can hear my voice and the piano plus any band or backing track that is playing. It means I can still hear the audience and their reactions. Lots of my friends in this business have told me how amazing in-ear monitors are though. These are the headphones that you often see pop stars pulling out of their ears, letting them hang around their necks in stadium shows. They need them in when they're singing to hear themselves over the screaming fans, but when you're speaking to the audience they can be very distracting. Try putting your fingers in your ears and then speaking. That's kind of what it feels like and it's very alien if you've never used them before.

I was told just before the first rehearsal that I'd be using them and I didn't know at the time that I could say no. The battery pack was clipped to my trousers under my suit jacket and the cables ran under my shirt and suddenly a man's voice was in my head asking if I could hear him. I said I could but I didn't know who, or where he was. He told me his name and that he was the sound guy. Figures. Then it was down to the studio floor for rehearsals.

After some discussion, the costume department made me a cool jacket for the show. It was white with the words 'Music', 'Funny', 'Family', 'Laughter' 'Piano', 'Comedy' and 'Baldy' printed in black on one side. You get to keep whatever costume they give you so I was pretty happy with my custom jacket. On the studio floor, I immediately hated the in-ear monitors. Even though there wasn't actually a live audience to hear, and wouldn't be for the actual show either, I couldn't shake the feeling that I was just singing to myself. It was going to be hard enough trying to muster whatever extrovert, performing spark I can make appear under normal circumstances, but when I was confronted with a thousand small TV screens instead of real, live humans and the feeling that I was singing in a bathroom, not to mention the anxiety of performing to millions of people in a TV studio, something else that I had never done before, I was, to put it mildly, shitting myself.

We ran through the song a couple of times and some of the photos that I had sent to Beth magically appeared on the piano as I was singing. It did look lovely. I had also told her that I would need to walk to the piano instead of already being sat in place as I wanted to use my car-unlocking gag at the beginning where I point my 'keys' at the piano, a beep is heard and I can then lift the lid. I was keen to show that I wasn't just limited to being the Piano-Man but could do some funny 'bits' too, having decided not to use the tape measure gag in my audition. I'd also rehearsed the end of the song where the backing track comes in and I planned on standing in front of the piano for the big ending and the dramatic last note which thanks to

Anni, the vocal coach on the show, I now had every confidence in being able to hit.

After a couple of run-throughs, they asked me if I could stay sitting at the piano for the end as it would look better on camera. I was reluctant, mostly because I hadn't actually rehearsed playing the piano for the end of the song but again I didn't realise I could say no so I quickly ran through the chords that I would need to play. They also asked for a couple of changes to the lyrics, just a word here and there which I was a bit pissed off about. They'd had a copy of the song for months now and I'd rehearsed it every day. The lyrics were almost muscle memory by now so having to remember to change a couple of words was extra stress that I didn't need. I did manage to say no when they suggested I cut the car alarm gag though. I'd used that in my stage show many times and I knew it was a good laugh. As I was going to be singing a pretty nostalgic song I felt it was essential to set the tone at the beginning that I was still very much a comedy performer. As soon as I insisted that it stay in, it wasn't a problem and I realised that perhaps I had more creative control than I thought I had.

So no live audience, horrible in-ear monitors and new last-minute lyrics and chords that I hadn't rehearsed. All of these explanations are just excuses for my confession that when it came to the actual recording of the show the next day, I screwed up. Big time.

Anni the vocal coach is just lovely and helped me considerably with my breathing techniques, not to mention learning the song. I've never had any singing lessons in my life, in fact, I only started singing professionally in my twenties when I was working as a lounge pianist at a hotel. I was a big fan of songs by composers like Rogers and Hart, Cole Porter, Gershwin, Irving Berlin etc. and as well as beautiful, timeless melodies, the lyrics to those old songs are often pure poetry. I would learn to play the tunes by memorising the lyrics and singing them in my head as I played the melody on the piano. One evening at the hotel I was explaining to the audience the genius of Lorenz Hart as a lyricist using 'Ten Cents A Dance' as an example.

"Sometimes she thinks

She's found her hero,

But it's a queer ro-

Mance."

That's a great bit of mid-word rhyming. This is the same guy who wrote My Funny Valentine, The Lady Is A Tramp and my Grandpa's favourite 'Bewitched, Bothered and Bewildered. I say his favourite, I'm not sure it was but it's one of my favourite stories that when he was working at Barclay's Bank, he was invited to a posh black-tie dinner. Knowing that he was a great singer, one of his co-workers persuaded him to get up and sing with the band. Unfortunately, Grandpa had been availing himself of the free bar so thought it would be funny to change the lyrics and sing 'Bewitched, *buggered* and bewildered'. Not a huge deal these days but in 1949 in a posh ballroom with bank executives, it didn't go down too well.

After waffling on about these great lyrics someone in the audience suggested I sing it and that was the first time I sang in public. Then you couldn't shut me up. I started writing my own songs but that was usually just to get a laugh so the actual art of singing was secondary in my mind. Now I'd written a song that required a last note right at the top of my range and Anni was there to make sure I hit it. Hers was also the only other voice that I could hear in my in-ear monitors other than the sound guy during rehearsals. It was a slight comfort and almost drowned out the other voice in my head telling me I was shit and what was I hoping to achieve?

We had one more rehearsal before the actual recording and the rules were very strict: even though the show wouldn't be live, it was still a competition so I had to pretend that it *was* live and I could not stop mid-performance under any circumstances. Usually, if you're recording a TV show and something goes wrong you can stop and start as often as necessary until you get it right but that wouldn't be fair in a competition. I'm not sure I could *ever* do a performance and think 'Yup, nailed it' so I had to be happy with getting it as right as possible the first time, as you would in a live show except this was a live show but with no live audience. Just live TV which I had zero experience of.

I walked onto the studio floor for the final rehearsal only for a producer to ask if I had another jacket. I was wearing my custom one with the black print as I had the day before but Simon had seen some footage of the rehearsal at home on his sick bed and didn't like the jacket. He was still running the show even with a broken back. A runner was dispatched around the London shops to find me one... on a Saturday afternoon!

The rehearsal went well. All the acts had been given our marks on the studio floor to show where to stand when we were chatting to the judges and where we should move to depending on who was chosen to be in the final top three. This was a new aspect of the show introduced that year where the judges would select their top three acts and then one of those would be selected to be the Judge's Choice to go straight through to the final without having to wait for the public vote. I had been at the back of the crowd of performers when the marks on stage were being pointed out so asked the floor manager afterwards to repeat the instructions. When I asked where I should move to if I wasn't one of the judge's top three choices I was told I wouldn't need to worry about that. To this day I don't know if he was just being kind and complimentary about my song or if there had been a backstage discussion with the judges and I was always going to be one of their choices. It's a common question about the show whether any of it is 'rigged' and I never got any inkling about any manipulation other than that one comment so I still don't know but I'm also not complaining about it.

All the photos of my family were now arranged to appear on the lid of the piano at the appropriate moment during the song. I'd learnt the ending on the piano, the new lyrics were in and so were the in-ear monitors which my brain hadn't accepted yet but I was a professional and so gave myself a stern talking to and convinced myself that I could nail this.

I watched the opening VT and my song 'Long Time Coming' on the huge screen at the back of the stage as I stood in the wings and then it was time to walk onto the studio floor. The car alarm beeped as I pointed my keys at the piano and hundreds of tiny faces on tiny television screens visually laughed but audibly there was nothing. Very disconcerting. I started my song and the first photos appeared on the piano. Cameras were everywhere. Some on shoulders as you would expect, a couple on cranes that were swinging and dipping all around me, and one in the middle of the virtual wall that I was told I should focus on. It was all going quite well and I may have relaxed slightly, or I may have caught Amanda's eye, or I may have been thinking about the five stitches on the side of my head where my mole used to be worried that my stitches would be shown in high definition across the country, despite the director assuring me that they would only film my good side. The mole had been removed a week earlier and I was still waiting for the results from the biopsy. Perhaps it was the sensation that I was singing to myself in a bathroom or it could just be that I'm an idiot. Any of these things could have put me off my stride because even though I wasn't playing Chopin, I'm not Victor Borge and the result was that I suddenly found myself singing the wrong words.

Well, they weren't the wrong words per se, they were just the wrong words at that point in the song. There were two moments in the number where I played the same accompaniment on the piano: once in the middle and once near the end. As my fingers were relying on muscle memory and were busy playing what they knew they should be, my brain had slipped a gear and my mouth decided to sing the words at the end of the song. I realised immediately and everything seemed to slow down. A slight cliché I know but true, as most clichés are, hence them being clichés. (I'm just chuffed that I've found how to type that little symbol above the é.) I frantically tried to remember the lyrics that I should be singing and then tried to think if I could substitute them. Would it make any sense when the wrong photos appeared? Could I just repeat this bit at the end of the song? Had anyone noticed? I knew that I couldn't stop. That had been reiterated over and over again and other acts before me hadn't had that opportunity either. If I stopped, I guess legally they would have to still broadcast it. I may be able to start again but I was past the halfway point so that would be a bit shit. Then there were the hours of production rehearsals that the team had done to ensure that the right photos would appear at the right time in the song, all of that was ruined. All this is flashing through my mind as I realise that I'm now singing the end of the song! I've cut about two minutes out of my four-minute performance. I have no idea what photos are being shown, I'm too busy holding back the emotion as I realise that I've screwed up this huge opportunity. I'll just get to the end and hopefully hit the big note and that will be that. If you watch it back on YouTube, there is a very subtle moment you can spot when I realise what I've done. My eyes widen very slightly as my arse cheeks clench shut fast. You can't see the arse action but trust me, it happened. Everything tensed up. A bead of sweat formed at the top of my spine and I felt it trickling down my back.

    I managed the last note and faked a smile as I leapt up from the piano… only to see the judges leaping up too. That really threw me. They're all clapping. The tiny people on the tiny television screens are all clapping too. I cross to my mark to chat with the judges and join Ant and Dec at an anti-social distance (why was it called social distancing? We showbiz luvvies like a good hug and multiple cheek-kissing. Nothing social about standing two metres apart and air kissing. Just a bit awkward.) The boys seem over the moon with my performance but they're professionals, the cameras are on and I have no doubt that even if they were mortified at my performance they would be able to hide it. I just look a bit confused. Then even more confused when David Walliams says:

"Well, we need another golden buzzer! That was just brilliant." And the other judges go on to say the loveliest things. Ashley Banjo announces that we could be looking at the overall winner of the show. Ant and Dec realise at this point that I don't seem to be taking it all in and suggest I'm a little overwhelmed. I tell them I am, for so many reasons. The comedian/over-sharer in me is tempted to just blurt out what had happened. That I'd cut half the song out, including some really funny, poignant and clever lyrics that I had spent months rehearsing. But then it gradually dawns on me that because the song is original and none of the judges has seen any of those months of rehearsals, they don't know. I may have totally got away with it. I mean the Director must be spitting feathers after the hours of preparation. What was the language being shared down their headsets when I decided to change the song as I was singing it? How did they even manage to improvise well enough with the photos to cover my mistake? I've never had the opportunity to ask them, but whatever they did had worked and I left the studio floor very bewildered and very emotional.

I didn't realise quite how emotional until I saw Anni standing there. Being one of the people who knew the song as well as me, or probably better as it transpires, she held her arms open and ignoring all social distancing protocol, I fell into her ample bosom and sobbed my eyes out. Looking back it was mostly relief but also I was so mad at myself for screwing up. I hold myself to a much higher expectation when I'm on stage having been doing it for so many years. I was upset that I hadn't performed the song as I'd written it, I was angry at my unprofessionalism and I was relieved that the judges had still enjoyed it, and it all came out against Anni's silk blouse.

Then I couldn't stop. Looking back I was definitely functioning in the shadow of my health worries anticipating that a thirty-year-long fear of cancer disrupting my life was about to come to fruition combined with the worries that lockdown brought with it. We were on the last dregs of our overdraft and I had accepted a bounce-back loan of £15,000 which would give us some breathing space but other than that, we had nothing. As a self-employed entertainer who hadn't performed significantly in the UK for over twenty years, my prospects were dodgy at best. Cruises had shut down and they had been my staple income for a long time and our savings for a rainy day were not going to stretch to a rainy year or longer. At the time I wasn't acknowledging any of this but it was certainly being expressed that day as I walked away from a soggy Anni and into the studio car park where I just couldn't stop crying.

There were a few more acts still to perform before we all had to gather on the studio floor again for the judges to choose their top three acts to be considered as the Judge's Choice. I eventually made my way back to my dressing room and managed to call Emmah who was watching the show live on one of the tiny TV monitors on the virtual wall. Of course, she had known immediately what had happened and has confessed to me since that she was mortified as she watched it unfold but as usual if one of us is losing the plot, the other manages to talk them down off the ledge. So it was with red but dry eyes that I returned in front of the cameras accepting that even though the judges had said such lovely things, I didn't deserve to be even in the top three. Therefore it was with an even more bewildered expression that I was left standing there with Belinda Davids, the Whitney Huston tribute singer, and Jasper Cherry, the young magician, as the chosen top three acts. David and Ashley both voted for me to be the Judges Choice, Alesha voted for Belinda so the deciding vote came to Amanda who said she had to vote with her heart and choose the act that had reduced her to a blubbering mess that evening, and she chose me. When the cameras were off I did get the opportunity to tell Amanda just who the blubbering mess really was and what had happened during the performance. She suggested I should never tell anyone. So let's keep all this just between us, ok?

It was the 5th of September 2020 when this fourth semi-final was recorded. The episode was due to be broadcast three weeks later on 26th September and then the finals were scheduled for 10th October. In the meantime, I had another song to write and a mole's biopsy to wait for. It was going to be a dramatic few weeks.

CHAPTER 8
Diagnosis
Sept 2020

The consultant at the skin clinic was a large chap with small, round glasses that emphasised the size of his head. He seemed even bigger when he pulled his chair up close enough that I could count the hairs in his nostrils. Peering over the top of his too-small spectacles, he looked me right in the eye, lowered his voice to almost a whisper and dramatically revealed that they had done a biopsy on my mole. I've got to be honest, at this point I could only think of the joke:

Doctor: I'm afraid it's bad news Mr. Jones. You don't have long to live.
Mr Jones: Oh my god! How long?
Doctor: Ten.
Mr Jones: Ten? Ten what?! Years? Months?…
Doctor: Nine, Eight, Seven…

Such was the gravitas of the consultant's manner, surely he was about to reveal my expiration date.
"Mr Young, I'm sorry to have to tell you…"
Another cliché and another opportunity to use é, but again, everything slowed down. At least that's how I remember it.
"…that the mole was cancerous. It was a melanoma"
I waited for the next bit, the number ten, or hopefully a bit higher, but he'd stopped speaking and was just staring at me with that fake compassion that some people can turn on. A bit dead behind the eyes but with the eyebrows slightly furrowed. If you've ever listened

to Jeremy Vine on Radio 2 when he's talking about something tragic, imagine that forced tone of compassion.

"Ok," I replied. "So what does that mean? What's next?"

"Well, it means you need to have a larger area around the site of the mole removed, approximately 10cm across, to see if the cancer has spread and then you'll need a skin graft. It will result in a slight disfiguration of your skull. You'll have a 5mm dent in the side of your head. People will stare at you and point, laughing, as if they were visiting a freak show. But it's not all bad news. At night when you lay on your side, your wife could use it as a tiny, shallow fruit bowl, perhaps for a grape or two."

Obviously I've paraphrased him a little. The dent was only expected to be 3-4mm so he'd exaggerated. Bastard.

Honestly, I'd have been happy if he *had* made a joke but that's me, giving bad news makes me laugh. It's quite a common reflex and a coping mechanism but of course, he'd stopped at the skin graft bit while the eyebrows remained compassionately furrowed, waiting for my reaction. I was quite matter-of-fact, slightly relieved that it wasn't worse news and slightly pissed off that he'd made me think it was going to be. His manner was so overly dramatic and serious that I felt the need to start joking to try and relieve *his* tension, not mine, but I didn't. I asked about the timeline and how long I could expect to wait for the operation and then immediately started to panic when I realised it could clash with my new TV opportunity. I wouldn't want to delay the operation in case it *had* spread and we needed to start treatment but then again, BGT wasn't going to wait for me. Oh god, this could become my 'story' after all. We all know how much Simon and his team love a good backstory on the show and if it's cancer, all the better. Imagine the ratings, the news stories, the triumphing and the celebrating when it's all over. I quite liked the idea of that last bit but the thought of it becoming what defined me on the show was almost as scary as the cancer itself.

I've been in showbiz my whole life and we all hope for that break, that one big opportunity and it looked like this could be one for me. Very unexpected at this late stage of my career. I'd resigned myself to continuing to work in a business that I am passionate about, doing a job that I know I'm good at and that I truly love with the bonus that it brings pleasure to people and makes them feel happy. The only downside was that I was spending weeks away from home and had reached my maximum earning potential which was really only covering expenditure with just a little left over for a few luxuries here and there and it wasn't going to change. Well, Covid looked like it was going to change it but not for the better so hopefully my new television exposure would help counteract that. There's no way I wanted cancer to become part of my 'image' where the public was concerned. I'd never know if people were voting for me because of my talent or out of sympathy. I was also immediately wondering what I was going to tell Emmah when I got home.

Emmah's Dad, Neville, had passed away the year before we met from a late-diagnosed melanoma. It had started on his finger but it was discovered too late and his illness and suffering had affected Emmah irreparably. On the drive home, I went over the different scenarios in my mind. Emmah knew everything up to this point and knew I'd gone to speak with the consultant so would be waiting to hear from me. I had three options:

Option 1: I walk into the house and tell her it's all fine. The mole was benign and there's nothing to worry about. Then I have to keep subsequent hospital visits a secret and try to hide any emotions that I may be feeling. Not really an option and one I'm actually very glad I didn't choose considering how quickly another minor deceit fell apart the following year.[1]

Option 2: I tell her that they need to do some more tests so have to remove more of my scalp. In other words, I don't need to say that the mole was a melanoma. For some reason that seemed like a good idea. I didn't want her to associate my situation with what she went through with her Dad. This was my first choice.

Option 3: Arrive home, see the wonky, fun-house wall that Dave, the one-eyed bricky has built to replace the garage door, walk in the house, see Emmah's concerned face as she's standing there in the kitchen, break down in tears and tell her everything and then sack the brickie. Not my first choice but the one that happened. I blame Dave.

---

[1] [SPOILER ALERT] In 2021 on the other side of my cancer experience and with some cash in the bank I began a motorcycle riding course with the intention of getting a bike. Knowing Emmah would be very much against this I decided to not add to her anxiety and failed to tell her. She also never asked, so I never had to tell a direct lie, just a few little ones; like I was going to a meeting with my accountant rather than an hour's motorcycle training. I managed to pass my CBT with this sort of deceit but was rumbled at my theory test when a friend's son was in the line behind me and word got back to Emmah. Rather than reveal to me that she knew everything, she went along with my deception while convening girl's meetings with the wives next door to discuss my impending doom. Announcing to them that I was cheating on her, pausing for their horrified reactions then adding "with a bike!" I mean how deceitful is *that*?! What happened next tells you everything you need to know about my wife: when I passed my test she had a huge bunch of flowers delivered to the house with a card that read: 'Congratulations on passing your bike test. Now stop fucking lying to me.'

Dave was taking the piss. He'd had to ask Emmah if I had a spirit level he could borrow. What kind of bricky doesn't own a spirit level??? Turns out Dave is a plasterer but he's been bricklaying for over five years and according to him he has some very happy clients. None of whom I'd contacted before hiring him. Then he tells me his story. His Mum died from cancer a few years ago so he'd started fundraising for various cancer charities and one of those events was a boxing match which he'd enthusiastically signed up for despite having no boxing experience. Similar to someone signing up to build a wall with very little experience of being a bricky. In his first round, he took a punch to the face which irreversibly detached his retina leaving him blind in one eye. The mother of his kids had recently left him so he was doing his best to raise them himself with various building jobs but it was difficult as he wasn't allowed to drive as his profiterole vision in his one good eye wasn't great either. His Dad had dropped him off that day and he would have to get a bus home.

I've got to be honest, it was a heart-wrenching story and I consider myself a pretty empathetic guy but I could not tear my eyes away from the wavy design that Dave had decided to go for in building my garage wall. It was shocking. An untrained eye, singular, could tell that this was not a good job but I was in a difficult position. I had only paid him half of the agreed amount and I'd offered to give him a lift home when he'd finished so for now I kept quiet intending to get a professional to look at it and help me with the necessary vocabulary to express my displeasure and suggest how it could be fixed. Our neighbour Kiel called his Dad who has a building company and he agreed to come and take a look the next day.

After a tense, silent car drive, I dropped Dave at his house and when I got home I found Emmah upstairs in our bedroom. I took off my shoes and suddenly found myself short of breath. I sat on the edge of the bed as the room began spinning and I broke out in a sweat. My heart started crashing against my chest as I barely managed to articulate what was going on; which was I was convinced I was having a heart attack. Emmah calmly sat next to me, put an arm around me and informed me I was having an anxiety attack.

"Don't be ridiculous," I admonished, "I don't suffer from anxiety attacks."

That was more Emmah's area of expertise. Anxiety, panic attacks and depression have been part of her life since her Dad had passed away. Meds controlled the depression but she'd had a few nasty anxious episodes in the past and recognised it in me for what it was. She told me to try and control my breathing and it would pass. I felt incredibly emotional. Tearful, frustrated, angry and scared, simultaneously. After a few minutes, it did begin to dissipate and then my phone rang and Emmah answered it, it was Jamie. She said a quick hello and then handed me the phone despite me mouthing that I'd call back but she insisted and told me to tell him. I shook my head even as Jamie was saying hello but again I was instructed to tell him and we all know what to do when our wives instruct us to do something.

Emmah confessed many months later that she had surreptitiously texted Jamie while I was in the midst of my heart/anxiety attack and had asked him to call, simply telling him that I could do with a friend. She knew that I needed to talk it out and that perhaps she was a bit too emotionally involved for me to be able to express myself properly. I love that woman. Sure enough, Jamie talked me down, or up depending on your perspective and by the end of the call I felt I was back to being me. I love that man too.

What a strange, alien, discombobulating feeling whose only redeeming feature is that it justifies the term 'discombobulating' which along with serendipitous, is one of my all-time favourite words. (Two others are 'plinth' and 'plethora'.) I also called my doctor and arranged an appointment to be prescribed some diazepam should another moment of anxiety decide to intrude on my otherwise quite laid-back persona. This would turn out to be a huge help, along with hot baths and single-malt whiskey in the months ahead.

Looking back on my diary around this time, if it hadn't given me anxiety then, I would get it reading about it now. The next day Kiel's Dad came to look at the wall. He had trouble speaking at first while trying to stifle his laughter. Then he had to take a photo so he could send it to Kiel who was away fishing so he could have a good laugh too. Finally, he asked me if I'd done it myself. How did he know I wasn't actually quite a proficient brick-layer? I suppose if I had been, the wall wouldn't look like that because I *would* have done it myself. A few technical terms were explained to me between more guffaws of merriment and a few non-technical terms that I had already decided were quite apt long before consulting a professional bricklayer. Then I called Dave for a very heated exchange.

"So what are you saying? That you're going to pay me?!"

"What I'm saying Dave is that it's going to cost me more than that to fix this job."

"But I've got kids to support."

"And I've got a fucking window to support and I don't think your wall is going to manage it."

We agreed that I'd let him arrange for his dad to come and take a look. His Dad *is* a qualified bricklayer and sure enough, he agreed that the whole lot would need to come down and be redone. He also offered to plaster the entire room as part of the fee so I was happy with that.

The next day my episode of the semi-finals was due to be broadcast. Dermott at The Gillery had offered to host a viewing party with a big inflatable screen in the garden and a projector. We dutifully invited friends and family and we all settled down with plenty of time to spare, just as well as Dermott had failed to arrange any sort of speaker system. Now I know I'm a handsome man but this was going to suck if our pub audience could only see me but not listen to the song. Someone suggested we use their karaoke speaker from home and off they went to fetch it. It all got wired up with seconds to spare. I could only watch through the partially splayed fingers of one hand while the other hand fed beer into my mouth. I had no idea how my screw-up was going to come across on the broadcast. I knew the outcome was favourable but I could remember all too well my cold sweat and buttock-clenching at the time. Surely that would be noticeable, especially on a giant inflatable projector screen.

I had a couple of pints in me and maybe a whiskey chaser, or two, but I've watched it back, just the one time since it was broadcast, and even without the booze it's barely noticeable! I have no idea how they did it but you really can't tell. I mean, it was still excruciating for me to watch because I had intense flashbacks but if nothing else it gave me a great story for the tour. Every audience got an exclusive when I got to perform the whole song as it was meant to be with all the missing photos too. Silver linings and all that.

Two days later I was due to be on Heart FM with Amanda Holden and Jamie Theakston so it was an early start, up at 6am, live at 7am (though barely a-live. See what I did there?) and then Lorraine at 9am with another original composition that I'd rustled up a couple of days before which involved me starting the show in my dressing gown. All this was from my little home studio still in my lounge while the new plaster dried in the converted garage.

Emmah and I discussed it and decided we shouldn't tell anyone at all involved with BGT about my health situation. We had no idea who we could trust and even if we begged them to keep it quiet, as our parents or grandparents were told during the war… the walls have ears. I was on tenterhooks[2] waiting to find out if my operation was going to coincide with my BGT finals performance. It was a horrible situation not being able to tell the producers that I may not be able to do the show as scheduled but then be unable to tell them why. We decided to just wait it out. Hopefully, it wouldn't coincide and no one would be any the wiser.

It turned out that serendipity would again play a part. The original date for my operation was the end of September which although wouldn't clash with the finals, would mean that I'd have to hide a large blue sponge that would be stapled to my head after the skin graft. 'Luckily', I got Covid for the second time so the operation date had to be postponed. As a cancer hospital, Christies had a very strict policy above and beyond the NHS guidelines. You had to isolate for an extra week after the recommended ten days NHS guideline. I was told to wait for another letter. In the meantime my anxiety decided I was far too relaxed and calm about it all so planned a strategic attack which was launched at the beginning of October. Retaliating forces were mustered in the upstairs bathroom under the command of General Diazepam and Sergeant Single Malt, often in the confines of a warm bath. Plans were drawn up and then promptly forgotten as they melted away to a land of fluffy clouds, enveloping

---

[2] I never truly understood that expression so just googled it… I was surprised to read that it's as written above, 'tenterhooks' and not 'tenderhooks' as I had originally written before autocorrect changed it for me. This book may not be educational for you but it's doing wonders for me. It's the hooks used to stretch fabric on a 'tenter' which is a wooden frame, enabling the fabric to dry. It is stretched across the tenter and is therefore quite taut and tense, as you are if you are described as being on tenterhooks. Also the derivation of the word 'tent', a fabric stretched across poles. You're welcome.

fog and hazy recollection with The West Wing playing on my phone somewhere in the distance. Bliss.

As if sensing my soaring, potentially victorious anxiety levels, the hospital sided with them and combined forces with a phone call on October 5th telling me they were worried that due to the depth of my melanoma, they were concerned it could have spread further and suggested I allow a sentinel node biopsy when they performed the scalping and skin grafting. This would determine to a very accurate degree whether the cancer had spread any further than the site of the mole. My General and Sergeant both agreed this would be a good idea until they couldn't care less or give any more of a shit and took me with them. More bliss.[3]

I should take a moment here to be very frank with you about how this was affecting me psychologically. I wasn't handling it well at all. Since I was a kid I'd had a morbid fascination with cancer and I'm not entirely sure where it stems from. My Grandpa died from it when I was fifteen so maybe it began in earnest then, when it took over from my fear of being obliterated by nuclear war. The statistics were one in three of us would experience cancer in our lives, updated now to one in two. I was convinced that I would be one of those three and it would cloud my mind late at night imagining the disease inside me. Around the same time, I found a lump in my stomach which very nearly tipped me over the edge until it was diagnosed as a lipoma, a small cyst and quite harmless. Some people are more prone to them than others and I was to go on and discover many more in the years

---

[3] I'm not condoning the use of muscle relaxants, certainly not regularly and definitely not washed down with delicious single malt whiskey. It's a very comfortable habit to fall into and you can easily become addicted which is not good. Follow the advice of your doctor and try not to listen to what your General and Sergeant might be whispering in your ear.

to come. I had four removed from my lower arm when I was thirty-five as they were starting to look unsightly. Today I have about eight of them, most in my arms, a couple in my stomach and one on my back.

I've always had moles. They are a trait in my family and I've always been fair-skinned and very slow to tan. Luckily I am not a person who enjoys sunbathing or even really being in the sun, unlike Emmah who is only truly happy if she is baking in it and she tans in minutes. When I began travelling a lot for work, often to very hot and humid climates, I was always quite good at wearing sun cream. Being follically challenged from quite a young age and despite experiencing a sunburnt scalp more than once I was also quite good at wearing hats despite not being a naturally good-looking hat-wearer. You know those people who can manage to still look good in something as ridiculous as a deer-stalker hat (Sherlock Holmes) or a cowboy hat (any cowboy)? My face shape just doesn't suit headwear but it's better than a post-burnt head flaking dead skin everywhere. That's a much worse look than just me in a hat so I usually just suck it up.

Despite my good sun protection habits, I guess I wasn't careful enough and any one of those sunburnt scalps could have led to my melanoma diagnosis. Some statistics suggest that sun exposure earlier on in life leading to a blistering sunburn can increase your risk of skin cancer by up to 80% when you're older. That's a pretty shocking number and one that should ensure every parent protects their kids because they're not going to do it themselves. A beach is just a happy place for them and I know my boys can spend hours bobbing in the water on holiday where the sun's rays can be reflected and cause even more damage.

Now here I was with my very real fears coming to fruition. The hospital explained that my melanoma was at an intermediate depth of 2.8mm so they were concerned it may have spread and so my imagination ran wild. There weren't enough songs to write or TV shows to appear on to distract me enough from the thought of dying. Late at night, wide awake while Emmah slept next to me, (I originally wrote 'gently snored next to me' but deleted it. She doesn't snore. Ask her.) I would imagine having to tell my boys that I wouldn't get to see them grow up and fall in love, I wouldn't get to hold a Grandchild. It would bring tears to my eyes which would then become anxiety, my heart would race and I'd have to get up so I didn't wake Emmah. On more than one occasion I purposefully did wake her just so I could have a hug, and stop her snoring.

Cancer is never far from any of our lives. Many years before my diagnosis, Emmah's Mum, Gail had rekindled her relationship with her first boyfriend from before she had met Emmah's Dad. Steve was the loveliest of guys, a true gentle-man. Softly spoken with a weird obsession for his hair which existed only on the sides of his head. He and Gail had many happy years together before he too was diagnosed with terminal cancer. Having nursed her husband through his final months now Gail was going to do the same for Steve. It was truly heartbreaking. I was in awe of how brave and resilient Steve was during the last months of his life. I'm sure he had many moments of despair but I never saw it. We took a family holiday in a motorhome around Italy when Nathan was a baby and took Gail and Steve with us. He was in so much pain and often couldn't hide it when he stood up in the cramped living quarters but other than that you would never have known that he'd been given an expiry date.

One evening he and I were enjoying a beer together and I made him recount his favourite joke on video camera for posterity and I'm so glad I did. The memory of the first time we heard it still makes me smile. Emmah and I had a couple of friends visiting, Rachel and Warren, both of whom are larger-than-life characters. It was Sunday lunchtime and we were at our local pub where we were joined by Gail, Steve and a few other friends. As the drinks flowed we began telling jokes and the subjects got broader as the laughs got louder until there was a small silence and lull in the conversation when Steve quietly commented,

"I've got a joke."

He'd been very quiet up to this point not being a natural extrovert or particularly comfortable being the centre of attention. I couldn't remember ever hearing him tell a joke up until now and we all stopped to listen. He told it so well with such brilliant timing that it floored us all and remains one of my favourites up to this day. Unfortunately, it doesn't translate very well to print and it's also not very politically correct but you deserve to know it. (The speech impediment is printed here as a stammer but if you can also read it with a combined nasal twang I think it enhances the humour.)

A religious leader is holding a faith-healing session and has a large crowd before him. In a loud, confident, preacher-type drawl he exclaims:

"Does anyone have an affliction from which they need to be cured? Step forward now and praise the Lord. Have faith in Him and you shall be healed…"

A little old lady shuffles forward on crutches.

"I need to be healed," she pleads quietly.

"Little old lady," the healer continues, "Step forward and put your faith in the Lord Jesus Christ. He shall work his miracles through me and you shall be healed of your handicap. Do you believe in the Lord Almighty?"

"Yes I do" she confirms.

"Then step forward to these screens behind me. Go behind the screens and pray to Him that you may be healed and lose those crutches. We will raise His name to the Heavens and you shall be free to walk again unaided. By the power of the Lord Jesus Christ…"

The little old lady shuffles behind the screen and people in the congregation are crossing themselves and clasping their hands in prayer.

"Does anyone else here today need the healing power of our Lord and Saviour?" he asks.

A man steps forward and pleads with an obvious speech defect:

"Me… I n..n…need to be c..c…cured… pick me."

"You Sir… you have a speech defect. How long has this affected you?"

"All m…m…my life" he mumbles.

"Sir, go behind the screen with the little old lady and pray with her. You too shall be relieved of your handicap. Your speech burden will be lifted and you will be heard clearly by your brothers and sisters here today. Praise the Lord!"

"P…p…praise the Lord" he stammers as he walks behind the screen.

Then the preacher works the congregation up into a state of religious fervour as they are calling out Jesus' name, swaying with their arms in the air and praying at the tops of their lungs. After a good ten minutes of this he stops them with a wave of his arm and shouts:

"YES!! By the power invested in me by the Lord Almighty, I cure these people of their afflictions. Little old lady… throw your crutches over the screen!"

A pair of crutches are seen to clatter to the floor in front of the screens. The congregation cheer and praise the Lord. The preacher continues:

"YES!!! Praise be to Jesus! And now Sir…. Speak to us…" and the same nasal, lispy voice stammers:

"She's f…f…fallen over!"

I hope it works in print because I'm laughing again now typing it. Just a great joke that I'd never heard anyone else tell and I've hung out with some really good joke tellers. I think at the time the combination of no one expecting Steve to come out with a good joke along with his quiet, gentle demeanour made us roar with laughter for so long that our mouths and sides were aching. To this day the whole family uses 'she's fallen over' as a guaranteed moment of brevity in any situation. All thanks to Steve.

On what was expected to be his last Valentine's Day he wrote a card to Gail which simply said 'To my first love and my last'. It brings tears to my eyes today. I wanted to be that brave, that resilient. I wanted to have that sort of dignity but if I was falling to pieces like this before I'd even been given any long-term diagnosis, how was I going to cope if the worst news was to come? The thought of that just compounded my anxiety. Maybe it would be easier once I knew for definite, one way or the other. It would definitely be easier if I got the all-clear, I knew that much.

It was the Senior Nurse to my consultant at the hospital who made me acknowledge what was tearing me apart. Emma (note the same name as my wife but without the random h at the end of her name. A quirk that Gail bestowed on my sister-in-law Rowenah too) had been following my success on BGT and was quite a fan but very professional. On one of my visits, I confided in her that I wasn't sleeping well and had been prescribed Diazepam to help me cope with my anxiety. Emma was quick to point out that she wasn't surprised. This was the scariest health issue I had ever encountered but it was coinciding with the greatest moment in my career. I must have been feeling like I was being torn in half. My realisation that she'd hit the nail on the head opened the flood gates and I couldn't hold back my tears. That was exactly how I felt. I was drifting through my television experience in a bit of a haze, almost watching it happen to someone else while my mind couldn't be dragged away from how scared I was that I wasn't going to be able to enjoy my future with my family. Admittedly there is an extract from my diary on the day of the finals that says:

'These are the first two days in forever when I haven't thought about cancer.' So I was being distracted slightly it seems by the studio lights and the cameras.

Chapter 9

The Final

October 2020

How had I got here? Maybe I wouldn't have been feeling so retrospective had it not been for the pandemic and the whole world being thrown into disarray. I've been asked many times if BGT changed my life and it's an easy answer to say yes, which under normal circumstances I'm sure would be true. But it was Covid that changed mine and everyone's life. Being a part of BGT let me maintain some sort of normalcy while so many of my friends were having to do what they could to make ends meet. Whether that was working for the NHS, manual labour on a building site or even building a giant cobb wall around their property to increase the value of their home.[4] All the huge changes that BGT was bringing into my daily routine were very much overshadowed by the immense changes that this shitty illness was bringing to everyone around the planet. I think most people were questioning 'How did I get here?' when they were taking stock of their lives around October 2020, mine was just televised.

I'm also asked regularly if I ever thought I could win. My stock answer is no, not until I heard my name being said by Dec did it dawn on me that I was going to win. I was very prepared to come second to Sign Along With Us. But a review of my diary shows a few tell-tale entries that quite possibly could have been composed with my

---

[4] As achieved by one of my closest friends Pete Matthews. An incredible feat of strength and perseverance that helped him to keep his mind off the potential destruction of his career by Covid. I visited on a day when I was passing nearby and held his step ladder for him as well as passed him a few tiles. I think between us it was quite an achievement to build that wall.

General on hand or even my Sergeant *in* hand but they show that at times I did question if I actually might stand a chance. My team around me were fairly convinced it seems. Jo Allen my Manager would regularly tell me that I was going to do it but that's what Managers are for isn't it? Jamie said more than once that I was in with a very good chance and he even put his money where his mouth was along with our mutual friend Pete, his only mistake being to let Pete arrange it and he ended up betting less money with less favourable odds but they still made a few quid on my success which I'm very happy about.

So on 7th October, I find myself on a train to London to rehearse the Finals show the following day and then record it on 9th with the live results on 10th. The lineup consisted of the five Judge's Choice acts: Myself, Nabil Abdulrashid, a standup comedian who was Alesha's golden buzzer act, Aaron and Jasmine a dance duo, Steve Royle, a comedian and juggler and Magical Bones… I think he was an opera singer. [citation needed][5]

We were to be joined by the five acts chosen by the public vote, four of which proved that magic was still very popular: Aidan McCann an eleven-year-old Irish magician, Damien O'Brien, a thirty-four-year-old magician (not Irish) James and Dylan Piper, a Father and

---

[5] Firstly, this is a visual joke courtesy of Wikipedia. I wouldn't usually point that out but I have this footnote available so thought I may as well. The real reason for the footnote is I'm sat typing this on the new Celebrity cruise ship 'Beyond' that I've joined, principally to perform my new show but also to get this book written without the school run getting in the way. I typed the sentence above along with the cheap Wikipedia visual joke, walked off to get a cup of tea, came back and WALKED INTO MAGICAL BONES!!! I didn't even know he was on board the ship! Whats that all about?! Going to take a break now to recover. That is really weird.

son magic act, Jasper Cherry, a fourteen-year-old magician and Sign Along With us, the choir created by Jade Kilduff with her brother Christian to promote sign language.

Seriously, thank god[6] and Beth's budget and space issues that I wasn't going to levitate a piano. Hell, I wasn't even going to mention that I used to perform magic. I couldn't work out if the plethora of magicians (There needs to be a collective noun specifically for magicians. I've been to enough magic conventions to think of a few) was a help or a hindrance. The public obviously loved magic as most of them had been voted through whereas no one had voted for me to be there. But then if you were one of five magicians competing in a variety show, the pressure was on to do something different. No one wants to see another deck of cards however good the last four card tricks have been. Maybe that would work in my favour and I couldn't help analysing it.

All of us were put up at a hotel near the LH2 studios but it was a strict timetable for recording the program to limit interaction and any possibility of covid contamination so it was quite a lonely experience despite the hundreds of crew that work on the show. My experience of being backstage at any show is the fun of jumping between dressing rooms and sharing the nerves and anticipation with other performers but it was very subdued on the dressing room level. Everyone was masked and we were told we absolutely could not leave our dressing areas unless required to. Kind of took some of the fun out of it and just left me to overthink the lyrics to my song. Until the semi-finals, it had never crossed my mind, in over twenty years of performing, that I would ever forget the lyrics to a song. Mainly

---

[6] Any reference to any god in this book will be a small g owing to my devout atheism. Also due to not wanting to offend any of the other gods, not just the christian one. Not that they exist either. Note also the small c in christian.

because if there was a song I was even slightly unsure about I would stick the words on the top of the piano. Just knowing they were there was a crutch even if I never used it. For example, Mr Bojangles was a regular number in my stage shows as my little tribute to one of my heroes, Sammy Davis Jr. I have loved the song since I first heard it when I was about ten years old but when I started to do shows, firstly I was too young to sing the song (I think it works better if you've got some experience under your belt) and then it was too daunting to do a song that had become such a trademark for Sammy. I certainly could never perform it standing up. What would be the point? I'm never going to better Sammy's version. So I had an arrangement written for piano and band and made a little video tribute to Sammy to play on the theatre screens as I was performing it. As the video relied very heavily on me getting the lyrics correct and in the right order, I always had them on a piece of paper on the top of the piano. I can honestly tell you that I never once looked down at those lyrics... until the day they weren't there. I'd forgotten to set them before the show and as I confidently began the song, I remembered that I'd forgotten them (is that an oxymoron?) and looked down to where they should be, seeing they were not there and simultaneously completely forgetting where I was in the song. Again, the brain is a marvellous and sometimes frustrating organ. There are others.

 I had suggested to Anni that they let me use an autocue system or even stick the words on the piano but that kind of thing is frowned upon in competitions apparently. I was tempted to sneak them in anyway but instead, I had the novel idea of just learning them... and not using in-ear monitors.

 As I mentioned earlier, the song was a rewrite of the floating piano idea 'Up In The Air', and I'd worked with Steve Dunne again to polish it. He has a great talent for editing. We managed to get the song cut from five minutes to less than four without losing any of the content. I'd had a couple of Zoom meetings with Beth to discuss the look of the stage. I'd asked for a giant flag to be unfurled with the words 'Britain's Talent Will Be That We All Carry On' and sure enough, it pretty much filled the stage. They asked me if I wanted to keep it after the show but where the hell was that going to go? I didn't even have a garage anymore.

Beth's other idea was a black and red theme with the black piano being lit with red lights from underneath. I quipped 'Ooh, like a Christian Louboutin piano!' For those of you not into your designer shoes, Louboutins are the stupidly expensive ones with the famous red soles. They often incorporate crazy spikes somewhere in their design and even though I'm not a designer label kind of guy, they do look pretty cool. Beth agreed that Louboutin was her inspiration for the look and I jokingly suggested I should wear a pair for the show. Without missing a beat, Beth agreed! Knowing that we got to keep our costumes, I was very happy. I think Emmah was more excited than me and immediately began searching for the perfect pair online. We found some red, black and white ones with metallic flashes down the side and spikes on the toes. That could help with social distancing. They were pretty awesome, as they should have been for £900! Even if I didn't win the show and the £250,000, I had the most expensive pair of shoes I'd ever owned. A small consolation when we'd probably still lose the house while we drowned in post-Covid debt. I remember the costume guy telling me that I had a lovely image on the show as the down-to-earth family guy so maybe I shouldn't be wearing shoes that cost more than my mortgage. I laughed at the time but it would come back to haunt me.

I'd had all kinds of ideas for my song over the preceding few months. After the floating piano had been shelved and I'd rewritten the song, I thought the moment when I stood up from the piano (which I'd insisted on this time) just before the flag fell, it would look really cool if some military drummers could join me on stage. I knew just the ones too. The Royal Hospital School in Suffolk had been my home for seven years from the age of eleven and they had a fantastic marching band. How amazing would it be to involve them? It was a short-lived idea when I was told that due to Covid restrictions, we couldn't have any extra people on stage with me or in the studio. It was disappointing but I would go on to work with four of the drummers on the Royal Variety Show the following month but more on that later. (Sorry, another missed [spoiler alert]). However, there was a moment of rancour during rehearsals when I was watching Aaron and Jasmine's performance and suddenly they were surrounded by a dozen drummers! No point in making a fuss, it would just make me look petty so I kept quiet but chalked it up to experience.

It was a long day of hanging around. I'd been up at 7am to get to the studio for 8am as Lorraine was going to be doing a segment on her show about the finals and I'd been asked if I'd be happy to be interviewed along with Nabil and Aaron and Jasmine. So we were standing on the studio floor trying to look perky on live TV before we'd even had a coffee. Then there was an ITV news interview after lunch. I was getting texts all day from family members and friends saying that they hadn't received their emails confirming their access codes for the virtual audience but I couldn't worry about that. Stress that I didn't need.

I was the last act to be performing on the night so the last act to rehearse and I thought it went pretty well. A couple of vocal sessions with Anni gave me more confidence and more to think about; I'd never really focussed on where I'd breathed during a song before but apparently, that's quite important. We had more instructions about where to stand on the stage to chat to Ant and Dec and then also where to go if we were in the top three acts and then it was back to the hotel for a pizza delivery and trying to sleep. I may have bought a General with me to help with that.

Back to the studio the next day to record the show. I bumped into a good friend by the dressing rooms, Phil Hitchcock, a great magician who was there to help Damian with his act. Phil and I had spent many years working on the cruise ships together and it was slightly calming to see a familiar face from my previous life. Pre Covid and pre BGT.

Moments later, standing in my dressing room just minutes before I was due to be collected and escorted to the studio floor, one of the young runners appeared in the doorway with a message from the costume department:

"Hi Jon. I've been told that you'll need to give the shoes back after the show."

"WHAT?! Noooo! They're the coolest shoes I've ever worn! I thought we got to keep our costumes?"

"Sorry Jon, I'm just a runner passing on a message."

"B..b..but… they can't even return them for a refund. I've been wearing them for 2 days and my wife assures me that once the red sole is scratched they can't be returned."

"Again, I'm just the runner…"

"I don't understand. It's not like they don't have the budget! Why can't I keep them…"

"Jon…"

"Yeah, yeah. I know. Don't shoot the messenger. Or the runner."

I was disproportionately upset. They'd bought me Hugo Boss jeans, Reiss shirts and Converse for the semi-finals and two jackets, but now for some reason, I had to return these epic shoes that couldn't even be refunded. Hmmm… I smelt a rat but didn't have time to ponder it any longer as I was whisked away for the biggest performance of my life.

I felt that it went ok. Ant and Dec were very excited for their golden buzzer boy, the judges were all very kind and a few of the crew were very excited telling me that they thought I would win. I don't think I'd let myself get excited about it. I don't hide disappointment very well which is why I'm always relieved to learn that I haven't been nominated for any major awards. It would just be awkward. I was back in the hotel bar by nine o'clock chatting with Phil Hitchcock. For some reason, I confided all my recent health issues to him and he was a great listener. I probably talked his ear off knowing that I had someone who wasn't going to leak anything to the press so he got both barrels of all my pent-up worry and frustration. Sorry Phil but thank you for being there. It was a huge help.

I also got to meet Lee Martin who is the founder of Gag Reflex (isn't that a great name for a comedy management company?) the tour promoters who had worked with BGT performers in the past. He was keen to work with me on my UK tour the following year. It was a very strange conversation to be having but very exciting. I spoke to a few friends and family who had been watching on the virtual screen having finally got their access emails. Most of them seemed to be pretty pissed (If you're American, they weren't angry, they were drunk. Just one of many language differences that have caused me issues in the past. In one show, pointing out some of the many differences between the languages, I caused the wrath of two Trump supporters when I said that we have different words for different things like any two different languages. We say 'sweets', Americans say 'candy', we say 'petrol', Americans say 'gas'. We say 'negotiate', and Americans say 'bomb the bastards'. They made a formal complaint which I shall remember forever: 'Jon Courtenay made fun of the only world leader who is doing anything to solve the Muslim problem.' I rest my case) but they all said encouraging, lovely things. I was in bed by midnight and had no trouble sleeping. I couldn't change anything now, it was 'in the can' as they say. It did occur to me that this would be the first time I was put up for a public vote having been a golden buzzer at the audition and then the judges choice in the semi-final, so all I knew for certain was that the judges and Ant and Dec liked me. Tomorrow I'd find out if the public shared their opinion.

Chapter 10
Champion

There was an area created at the studios with a monitor and chairs where all the performers could sit together and watch the show being broadcast, which was lovely. A great feeling of camaraderie between us all and no pressure remaining although watching our performances back on the small screen was quite daunting and a real out-of-body experience. As it had been sat at home watching the broadcasts of the auditions and semi-finals. It's one thing to be in front of the cameras but then you see it edited with the music and the familiar logos and then your own silly face, it's a little weird. Even now if I watch a clip on YouTube I feel quite detached from it and that's not just down to the cancer distraction. Or maybe it is. I haven't been through BGT without the distraction so I have nothing to compare it to. It's like being asked by so many interviewers "What was it like winning the show during lockdown?" Compared to what? I haven't won it out of lockdown.

While the broadcast was taking place they were recording the halftime show in the studio and I snuck in to watch. It was the incredible musical medley of Mary Poppins, Les Miserables and Phantom of the Opera and was very poignant as theatres had been shut for so long. I wasn't really meant to be in there but it was dark and only a few people were standing nearby. After one run through I broke into spontaneous applause, tears running down my face with the joy of watching a 'live' stage production after so long and turned to the person standing next to me ready to apologise for my outburst especially as I wasn't even meant to be there. Luckily I stopped myself speaking just as I realised it was Sir Cameron Mackintosh! It was incredible that he'd managed to put this on at all with all the cast rehearsing and performing while remaining socially distanced. His impassioned speech at the end begging the Government to reopen the theatres brought another tear to my eyes and I needed a little make-up touch-up before I was back in the studio for the live results.

We were all on our marks for the countdown to the top three acts 'in no particular order' with the lights going dark on the seven acts who hadn't made it. All very dramatic and a little harsh if you ask me. Finally, it was me with Steve Royle and Jade and Christian from Sign Along With Us. Steve came third and got to say a brief but heartfelt message:

"If you're thinking about posting anything negative on social media this evening about any of us here tonight, we all came here for one reason: to entertain. We didn't come here to offend or upset people."

It was a well-thought-out proclamation, leaving out the fact that we were also hoping to take home the prize money! Maybe Steve was inspired to comment due to some of the flack that the stand-up comedian Nabil got as a response to his routines about racism and the black lives matter movement. He was telling me backstage that he'd received death threats, not just to him but to his wife and kids! Absolutely insane. I will never understand what drives these sad, pathetic people to hide behind their phones or computers and write this sort of bile. I'm not sure I could have brushed off *that* sort of rhetoric with a light-hearted song such as Baldy With A Buzzer.

Steve took his bow and I was left next to Jade and Christian. I was quite prepared to come second. I hadn't rehearsed my 'disappointed-but-happy-for-you' face and I was worried that my mic could pick me up saying "Bollocks" if I didn't win so I was concentrating on that, but more than anything, as dramatic as this sounds, it will give you some idea of how overwhelmed I had been by my cancer scare when I tell you that the main thought going through my mind in that interminable pause before the winner is announced was 'if I win £250,000, at least Emmah and the boys will be ok if I'm not here.' There was certainly a cloud hanging over me during what should have been one of the most exciting moments of my life.

My name was announced and I fell to my knees, my face buried in the palm of my hands as gold pyros and confetti exploded all around me. I know that because I watched it when I got home. Amanda was jumping up and down with joy and I was asked to speak. Stupidly but uncontrollably, I actually couldn't. I wasn't thinking straight so Ant and Dec turned to Jade who was in a much worse state than me but managed to at least thank everyone. Back to me and I waffled on about waking up that morning with the idea of a song in my head for the Royal Variety Show (true) then I had seconds to thank everyone at home and my family and express my hope that my Mum was still alive after all the excitement and then the credits rolled.

It was so frustrating not being able to hug Ant and Dec. We all just kept opening our arms and miming a hug with air kisses. However, as soon as the cameras were off Amanda rushed onto the stage and naughtily wrapped her arms around me for the bigger squeeze. It was so welcome, however against protocol it may have been. It's just a showbiz thing. We're very tactile, passionate, affectionate people and to go through that experience without being able to even shake hands was very strange. Thank you Amanda, I hope this hasn't got you in trouble. No more trouble than some of your outfits anyway.

Then it was a real whirlwind. I was whisked off stage for a photo in front of the judge's seats with the judges on either side of me. Ashley asked between photos:

"Are you looking forward to Monday?"

"Why?" I replied.

"You'll have a quarter of a million pounds in your bank account!"

"Really?"

I didn't think it was as simple as that. I know America's Got Talent has a weird payment system for their prize money having spoken to my friend Paul Zerdin, who won it in 2015.

"Are you sure?" I asked Ashley stupidly.

"I would know!" was his quick reply. Indeed he would.

It is a life-changing amount of money but again, I think it stopped my life from changing more than anything else and I will be forever grateful to Simon and the show for that. Then it was backstage for some more filming. They want to catch you on camera with that raw emotion from just winning so you're not given a moment to collect your thoughts. It was BGT's Instagram account, YouTube, then some press and everyone I'm passing from the crew is so happy for me and saying the loveliest things. All I can think is 'Where's my phone?!' We had to hand them to one of the crew as we walked on stage for the results and now I had no idea where it was. I wanted to speak to my family more than anything else so the person who was escorting me from pillar to post sent someone off to find it.

After about thirty minutes of interviews and photos, I got my phone back and managed to FaceTime Emmah and the boys who were all partying in our street two metres from all our neighbours around a roaring fire-pit. It was like a celebration of the Queen's Jubilee but without the bunting. Just as Emmah answered, Ant and Dec came out of their dressing rooms behind me so they video-bombed my call and the street's excitement level went up another notch. There's a screenshot somewhere and as blurred as it is, it's a lovely reminder of being able to share that incredible moment with my family.

Then a call to my Mum who *was* alive but incoherent. I thought my phone was going to explode with all the tings, bings, bleeps and vibrations that were coming through with notifications from everywhere. Another runner found me and said they'd escort me back to my dressing room so I could get my stuff. Alesha had mentioned after filming that the biggest disappointment about doing the finals during Covid was no after-party with Simon. He usually hosts a great gathering after the show and that's all that was missing really. Instead, it was back to my dressing room where I was confronted by my shoe-fetching friend already waiting for me.

"Ha!" I exclaimed… "I was hoping you'd forgotten." As I unlaced the sexy Louboutins and handed them over only realising then that I had nothing else to put on to replace them. Our costumes had been sent to the hotel so we could get dressed there.

"Oh," he paused, "Hang on… I'll go and find you something from wardrobe. What size are you?"

He came back with the most hideous pair of black office shoes that I've ever seen, and a size too big. I must have been grumbling as I handed over the designer shoes because as he left his parting shot was:

"You *have* just won a lot of money. You could buy your own!"
Cheeky shit.
To this day I'm convinced that the guy in charge of the wardrobe now has my shoes in his closet. There's no other explanation. They certainly weren't returned to Louboutin. Maybe he was just helping me to maintain my 'family-friendly, man of the people' image. That was kind of him.

Then I was leaving the studios, not feeling that different to when I'd arrived a few hours earlier. It sounds disappointing to even write that but it's true. Some guy called Jon Courtenay had just won the biggest talent show in the world. Good for him. Not sure how that affects me though. Why is that fat bloke walking towards me with a camera? He's shouting at me. What's his problem?

"Give us a smile Jon!"

I smile.

"Can you hold up one finger?"

"Why?"

"Cos you came first."

"Right-o"

That's the picture that was used in a few newspapers and magazines. It looks like I'm asking him to wait a minute before he takes the shot. Then I was in the taxi for the short ride back to the hotel. I don't think I phoned anyone or read any messages in that cab. I just sat there. Shell shocked I guess.

When the car pulled up outside the hotel there was a bit of a commotion in the lobby through the double glass doors. I wondered what was going on as I grabbed my bag and walked toward it. As I got closer I could see that it was most of Sign Along With Us, all crammed into the small lobby area between the outside glass doors and the reception area. As the outside doors slid open I realised they were singing and cheering, seemingly simultaneously. Presumably all buzzing from their second-place win. But no, they weren't celebrating their success, they were there to celebrate mine. All of them sang This Is Me as the smaller ones ran out and ignoring all covid protocols, hugged me or grabbed me all shouting my name and cheering me into the hotel as I frantically tried to find my phone to capture the incredible kindness and thoughtfulness of these fabulous kids. What a welcome. Most of the acts were still in the bar area along with the friends and family that they'd been allowed to bring because they were too young to be on their own. The first of many glasses was put in my hand and it was a lovely evening. At some point, I must have gone to bed.

The next day was the train home and I hadn't had my requisite eight hours of sleep. I'm that person that suffers if I only get seven so I try to get nine the next night. I know it doesn't work like that but I don't function well if I have a string of late nights and early mornings. I'm not sure that anyone does really. Except for my friend Pete. He's been called a sleep camel. He can go days on end with just a few hours of sleep each night, partying with the best of them and then just catch up with a good solid fourteen hours at the end of it.

I was on the train by 10am and at Piccadilly, Manchester just after midday where Emmah met me. That was a BIG hug! I confessed that I was exhausted, mentally and physically and would it be ok to have a nap when we got back. She said of course. We called in to see my Mum who was still incoherent and then finally pulled in to our close where the entire street was out, balloons were flying, banners were made and everyone cheered as I stepped out of the car.

"Well, what did you think was going to happen?" Emmah asked as I heard the pop of a champagne cork behind me. All of my extended family was there and it was fabulous. Much better than Simon's party would have been, and that's what I'll keep telling myself.

It was due to be a busy couple of days. A week earlier, Charlie Irwin, Simon's right-hand man on the show had asked if I'd be prepared to take part in the BGT Christmas Show should I win. It would be recorded at the Hammersmith Apollo and would be broadcast on Christmas Day after the Queen's Speech. I would be closing the show with whatever song I'd like to compose and then singing with Ant and Dec and the judges as dancers danced, snow fell and the credits rolled. It had never been done before but as the finals show was so late in the year, it seemed apt that they make a Christmas show featuring past performers and of course Santa. Naturally, I agreed and started to write some ideas for the song. The rehearsals and recording were scheduled for October 13th. It had originally been suggested that I stay in London after the finals show on the 10th but I'd insisted that I go home. There was no way I could wait another four days to see my family if I won it. Besides, the hospital had arranged my second Covid test for the 12th to ensure that I was fit for my operation which had been scheduled for the 17th. It was all working out perfectly. I'd managed to do the finals with my small scar barely visible and now I could do the Christmas show as well before the skin graft and head disfigurement. But you know when it feels as if all your ducks are in a row but then a shotgun blows them all in every direction…

The 12th passed in a bit of a blur. This Morning called again for me to be on and then it was a day of newspaper and radio interviews. I guess if it hadn't been for Covid I'd have been dashing between studios but as it was, Zoom was necessary and actually very favourable. I still wasn't installed in the new garage conversion as it still needed decorating so I wedged a chair under the lounge door to keep out eager kids and wives. Later that afternoon I was back at Christie's for the now-familiar nasal swab which had never got any easier and still made me sneeze and cough through watery eyes. Results would be back the next day, this was before any rapid testing was available so I was determined to remain very socially distanced from anyone on both the train journey to London the next day and for the recording of the show. I didn't want to jeopardise my operation date but then as we all know, the hand of fate can be a cruel one.

Chapter 11
Delay

I was on my train and London-bound early evening on the 13th of October, frantically learning the song that I'd written for the occasion. I was booked into a hotel for the night with rehearsals and filming all happening the next day. The lineup was great. Lots of familiar faces from the last fourteen years of BGT, a true variety show and I was going to be closing it. What a buzz. An hour into the journey my phone rang. I answered it with the traditional:

"Hi, this is Jon. I'M ON THE TRAIN."

"Hi Jon, this is Kat from BGT."

"Hi Kat. I'm on my way," I assured her.

"Ah. That's the problem, Jon. We've had to cancel it for now. There's been an outbreak of Covid amongst some of the production team and we can't make it work with such a reduced crew."

"Bugger."

Or words to that effect. By the time I got to London, it would be too late to get the last train back to Manchester so it was agreed that I'd go to the hotel as planned where a few of the acts were staying already, and then go home again tomorrow and wait for the rescheduled plan. It would mean covering up the skin graft on my head but I figured with it being a Christmas show, a giant Santa hat wouldn't look out of place.

It was late by the time I got to the hotel so I went straight to bed but in the morning it was lovely to see some familiar faces in the restaurant for breakfast, even the sour one of a previous contestant who felt that I'd stolen their thunder because we both played the piano! A real shame as we'd known each other long before BGT and I thought we were friends. I'm very pleased to say that apart from that one experience, I haven't had any negative feedback from friends or even acquaintances in the business at all since winning the show, just a lot of love and support. So here's a great big public thank you to every one of you.

I arrived home just after lunch in time for a phone call from the hospital.

"Mr Young, (my real name), did you attend The Christie for a covid test on 12th October?"

"Yes, I did."

"I'm pleased to tell you the result is negative."

"Fabulous."

"So just to confirm: Have you been isolating at home since the test was done?"

Let me confirm to you lovely reader that no one had stipulated that requirement at any time before or after my test. I should have just blagged it and said yes. I'd been so careful on my train journey and even seeing friends at the hotel there hadn't been a single hug. Not even an air kiss in anyone's direction. Some covid-laced daggers may have been sent in my direction from the previously mentioned envious party but I don't think they were contagious so I was confident nothing in my results could have changed. However, there had been a couple of socially-distanced selfies with a few people and I was aware that these could be posted online and it wouldn't take a skilled detective to summarise that I was lying so I stammered my reply:

"Um… well… the thing is, you didn't tell me I had to isolate…"

"Have you been to a shop? If it wasn't busy I'm sure we'll be ok, but we will need to retest you."

"Ah, ok. Not a shop as such but if you need to retest anyway… when would you like me to come in? My operation is due on the 17th."

"Can you come today? I know your consultant is keen to get your operation done."

Not as keen as I was, I can assure you. So it was back in the car and back to the hospital and back to coughing and sneezing in a small cubicle and then home again, this time to isolate, strictly, for the three days until I was due back.

They called the next morning.

My test had come back positive so my operation would have to be delayed.

Again.

I was devastated.

I'd spent so many sleepless nights imagining some bastard cancer cells running amok and I needed them to confirm it so we could blast the little twats with whatever shitty poison killed them before they nestled somewhere new and caused all kinds of trouble. Fuck. I called my GP and arranged a repeat prescription for the Diazepam.

Audition Day

Photo ©PND Photography

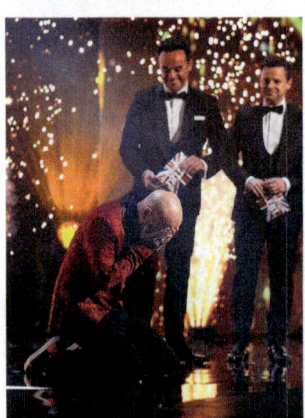

Photo © Thames/Syco/Freemantle

Photo ©PND Photography

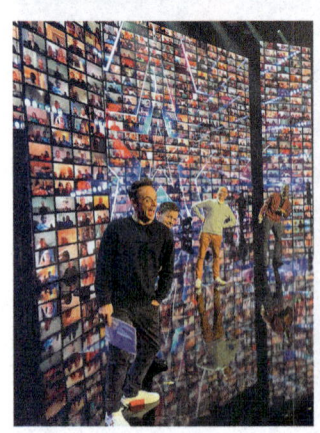

Photo © Thames/Syco/Freemantle

The models backstage at the NRTAs rushing to the window!

My home studio setup for This Morning

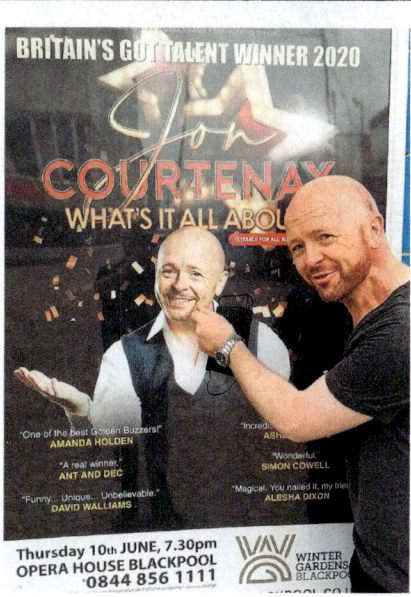

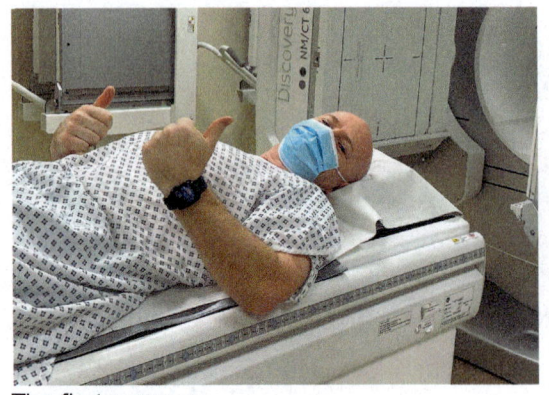

The first scan

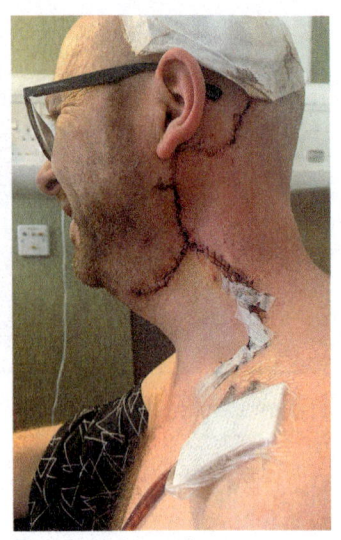

The 2nd operation

The first all-clear

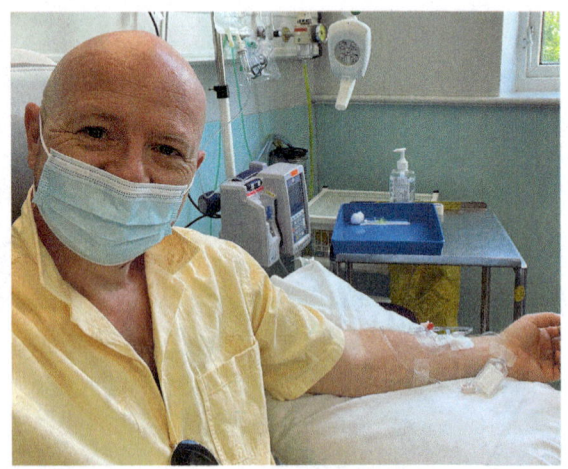

The last immunotherapy session

Chapter 12
The No-Royal, No-Audience, Variety Performance
Part 1

So far we'd managed to keep my whole experience out of the news. I'd decided that if they did the skin graft and the sentinel node biopsy showed that I was all clear then I'd come out guns blazing in support of cancer charities. I'd write songs, do shows, be an Ambassador and do whatever I could with this new platform that I had been given to help raise awareness. If on the other hand, it wasn't such good news, I wasn't sure how I was going to cope and perhaps not being in the public eye would be a good thing. For now, it was just a mental waiting game but it's not like I didn't have work to distract me slightly. The 'Rona as it had become known in our home, knocked me out a little. The usual aches and lethargy and the loss of taste. That was weird. I put it to the test eating lime pickle out of the jar with a teaspoon... nothing. Very strange.

On the 15th of October, I had my first Zoom meeting with the producers of the Royal Variety Show. That was surreal. They were absolutely lovely and made me feel like part of the team immediately, not just some guy who was only invited to the party because he'd won a competition. I guess in the past that may have been the case but they knew that I'd paid my dues for over 20 years and I expressed just how excited and privileged I felt to be a part of this historic show. It was one of a few programs that I had sat and watched with my parents for as long as I could remember. Dad was eighteen years older than Mum so between the three of us we had quite different tastes in films, TV and comedy but some things were always family viewing. Long before catch-up or on-demand, when there were just three or four channels to choose from, you could guarantee that on weekends you'd find the three of us watching

Morecombe and Wise, The Two Ronnies or Sunday Night at the Palladium. Then once a year, The Royal Variety Performance. There were other programs too. Dad was a big Fred Astaire fan and had his entire film collection on VHS. I loved watching him dance (Fred, not so much my Dad although he was a great mover too) it just looked magical. I was interested to read later in life when I was quite obsessed with performing magic that David Copperfield, the most famous magician in the world, wasn't inspired so much by other magicians as by people like Fred Astaire. There's also a wonderful story of Fred inviting Michael Jackson to his house to teach him the Moonwalk. Why was that never recorded for posterity? I was a young teenager when the American Film Institute hosted a special awards show to celebrate Fred's career. After numerous film clips and accolades from fellow entertainers, this old man walked onto the stage. I turned to my Dad and asked:

"Who's that?"

"That's Fred Astaire" Dad replied and I sat stunned into silence. This old, frail man with a wrinkled face couldn't be Fred Astaire. He was a young, dapper gent with smooth features and always dressed in a tailcoat. But it turns out he got old, and also that he hated wearing top hats and tailcoats. Further research revealed that he hated his large hands and long fingers too hence his habit of curling his fingers into his palm when he danced. I did love discovering that his first screen test had been a failure when the report read: 'Can't sing, can't act, can dance a little.' We insecure entertainer types cling to stories like this to help cope with every rejection we are bound to suffer during our careers. I may have dreamed of one day performing on the Palladium stage as Fred had done but never did I imagine that I'd be on the bill of the Royal Variety Performance. It was mind-blowing.

The first Royal Command Performance as it was called then, was in 1912 when King George V and Queen Mary were invited to attend a Music Hall Show at the Palace Theatre in London. It was meant to be in 1911, the King's Coronation year when the King announced that all profits should go to Variety Artiste's Benevolent Fund as it was known then, but the theatre in Edinburgh where it was due to be held burned down a month before the show was due to open so it was delayed until the following year. Since then there have been 92 performances.

The producers did warn me that it would be a bit different this year due to restrictions but the show most definitely would go on. The two biggest differences would be no live audience (I was getting used to that) and no Royal Family which was a bit of a disappointment I have to be honest. That lineup backstage after the show with the Royal party greeting the performers was such an iconic moment but one that I would sadly miss. For many years I had recounted my favourite Tommy Cooper story of when he met the Queen backstage after one of the Royal Variety Shows as told by Jimmy Tarbuck who was standing next to Tommy at the time:

"Your Majesty. Could I ask you a personal question?" (You're not supposed to do this.)

"Very well Mr Cooper."

"Do you like football M'am?"

"Not particularly Mr Cooper."

"I didn't think so. Could I have your Cup Final tickets please?"

It's become one of the most famous Tommy stories although John Fisher the magic historian suggests that Tommy 'borrowed' the line from Bud Flannigan who had asked the Queen Mother the same thing but let's not let origin get in the way of a great story. If not the line, Tommy had definitely stolen the show that year opening his routine by walking on stage with a sword and laying it on the floor with the handle pointing in the direction of the Royal Box quipping:

"Just in case!"

Sadly I wasn't going to get the chance to break any Royal protocols but I was still extremely excited. It had been scheduled to be at the Blackpool Opera House long before Covid was a thing and that turned out to be fortuitous as there is so much space backstage if you incorporate the Winter Gardens, so the full company of the show could easily maintain a social distance. I have no idea how it could have gone ahead at its regular venue, the London Palladium, where space is very limited hence BGT taking over the hotel next door. Plus Blackpool is only an hour from my home so I could get back after the show and sleep in my own bed instead of attending some crazy after-show party and having to turn down the advances of chorus girls. Because this was the 1920's after all.

I presume that under normal circumstances there *would* have been an after-show party that again I would be destined to miss, also I couldn't take any guests and once again the usual backstage atmosphere of dashing between dressing rooms wasn't going to happen. This was starting to be the norm and I didn't like it. There had been no word about when or even *if* the BGT Christmas show was going to be rescheduled so I had decided that the song that I was going to perform for that show would be much better suited for the RVP and it could be even more effective considering my plan:

In early December 2007, I was performing on board a small, exclusive cruise ship owned by Silverseas. It was rated a 6-star cruise line and prices reflected that. As I was always on board with guest status rather than crew it meant that I reaped all the benefits and also got paid to be there. You can understand why this was an attractive career and almost worth kissing my chances of fame in the UK goodbye for. All the drinks for passengers were included in their fare (so just free for me then) and the food rivalled any high-end restaurant anywhere in the world. I had my own butler although I never knew what to ask them for. I just told them I was working on board as well and if they ever needed a break they would be welcome to drop in, put their feet up and have a glass of champagne from the fridge in my suite. They would laugh politely and never once did they drop their butlering front. Far too professional. On top of all that, because the ships were much smaller than many of the other ones, we got into smaller, more exclusive ports. It's a fabulous way to see the world.

As was the case every year I was struggling to think of what to buy Emmah for Christmas. She insists that she is easy to buy for but I, along with most of her family, know that's just not true. One year I bought her a simple T-shirt as one of her smaller presents. Nothing designer, I think it was from Mango but it looked like something she would wear. When she opened it she couldn't hide her disgust. Or at least I was just good at sensing it. She admitted that it was hideous and that she would never wear it and since then I've very rarely bought her clothes. When I do it just reaffirms why I shouldn't because I still get it wrong. Just last year she had been complaining that since she had lost weight, none of her knickers fit her anymore so I went mad in Victoria's Secret and bought her a new drawer full and they weren't even all just for me. (As in they weren't all just sexy g-strings rather than I was intending to wear them.) I was fairly sure that the last knickers I had bought for her in the past had been mediums and if they were now too big, I would need to get small. Turns out I got it wrong and they were all too tight. Yes I know I could have gone through her underwear drawer and checked the sizes but the last time she caught me doing that there was an awkward conversation.

Then there was the year that she told me what she wanted; a short biker-style leather jacket from All Saints. Yes! I knew the shop having been told years earlier that it wasn't a store that sold sewing machines and I knew what a short biker-style jacket looked like. I spent an hour with the shop assistant who was a similar size and shape to Emmah asking her to try different styles on until I settled on a distressed leather one which both the assistant and I agreed was the nicest. Christmas morning, the not-cheap jacket is tried on and the verdict is she thinks it makes her look like a butch lesbian so it has to go back. (To all the butch lesbians out there… oh never mind. Emmah just didn't want to look like you. Hope you're not offended.)

So there I was with a few days to kill on a beautiful luxury cruise ship where I was sitting at the piano one day in the empty theatre preparing to practice some new song for my show and I had the idea of writing Emmah a song and making a little music video to go with it which I could give to her at Christmas. The best presents don't have to be the most expensive. As is often the case when I get a good idea in my head, the song came quite quickly referencing various times in our past when we were dating, influenced a little bit by Lily Allen's new album that I had been listening to. I called it Your Christmas Song and then spent a couple of days recording me miming it around the ship and at the piano so I could make a simple music video to go with it. I'd taught myself video editing when Nathan was born in 2005 and loved editing our home movies adding titles, soundtracks and sometimes special effects. We have a hard drive attached to the TV in our bedroom with every family holiday, Christmas, Birthday, Halloween and Easter egg hunt saved for posterity as a mini-movie and I love it when I catch the kids still watching them.

I finished the edit before I had to fly home and burnt it onto a DVD, (it was that long ago) made an insert for the DVD case, wrapped it and put it under the tree. On Christmas Eve when Nathan was in bed, Emmah asked if I wanted to open a small present and I thought it would be better to give the song to her that evening when she could watch it uninterrupted rather than on Christmas morning when we'd be accompanied by an excited 2-year-old. It was a huge success and when it had finished she gave me a huge hug and asked if this was going to be a tradition every year. I didn't miss a beat and said:

"Of course. Every year. A new tradition."

At least it was one present I knew I could nail.

Your Christmas Song

This is a Christmas song that you can listen to all year.
Written just for Emmah but it's something you can all hear.
Time to reminisce and think about days past;
Nearly ten years seem to go by so fast.

From Warner's Sinah Warren when you weren't taking chances,
You thought I was gay as you slagged off all the dancers,
Then you found out I was straight and it all got naughty,
Seven years later there's a baby Courtenay.

Chorus
This is your Christmas song,
With each other's the place that we belong.
We've stopped it all from going wrong,
Now this is your Christmas song.

I'd travelled so much while I was still single,
Going out to parties feeling free to mingle,

Met so many people who told me to slow down.
Then I met you and you joined me in the playground

I knew good times and said I'd show you them,
You knew you looked good up there on the podium.
All those sweaty hugs made me feel like a million
Quite a change from Warners to Styx and the Pavillion.
We won't mention me leaving or when we broke up,
Just that I needed a slap and I woke up.
Life then got just a little bit hectic:
Headaches, brain tumours, and a general anaesthetic.

29th Birthday on the Queen Elizabeth Two,
Didn't really know what present to get you,
We had a little chat and decided maybe
It would be sweet if I could give you a baby

Now it won't be long before our little boys arriving
At the gates of the school where you'll be driving.
Give him a hug and after he's kissed ya
We'll race home to make a brother or sister.

Now I know it's not ideal and I'm always travelling,
Sometimes it feels like your life's unravellin',
I've never been bothered that all my hair went,
But it would have gone sooner as a single parent.

That's why next year you've got to fly out to meet me,
A couple of ships and time in Tahiti.
I asked you to marry me five years ago in New York,
I promise very soon I'll prove it wasn't just all talk.

So if we're going down to Rio, gotta save my wages:
I saved money on your present but it took me ages.

I know it won't all make sense to you and you probably want me to expand on the brain tumour story but I'll let Emmah tell you about that in *her* autobiography. Suffice it to say it was a very shit time and the tumour is still in her head but it's benign and apart from the occasional splitting headache, she's OK. It did mean that for years afterwards if I was feeling at all ill, from the common cold to any minor aches or pains, she'd manage to dismiss it with "Well at least you haven't got a brain tumour." If nothing else my recent health issues at least let me match her trump card if not beat it. My scar is much bigger although if you meet her, she'll quite happily invite you to feel her hole and just before you embarrass yourself, she'll take your hand and guide it to the space in her skull that will never heal and is now a hole covered only by a thin membrane and her mane of thick hair.

For the next eleven years, I managed to write her a song, make a video to go with it and give it to her on Christmas Eve. Admittedly some were better than others. From that first, quite traditional love song I went on to dress up as Britney Spears in a school girl outfit for a parody of Oops I Think I Did It Again (Yes I know that's the wrong song for the outfit but if that's your only issue about me wearing a school girl outfit you need to address your priorities), a country song 'You're The Reason I'm Not Gay' which ended with me walking away from the camera with a guitar over my shoulder and a naked arse. Billy Joel's 'We Didn't Start The Fire' became 'I'm Just A Frequent Flyer' plus one of the weirdest entries, 'Christmas Will-e' which involved me singing a duet with a stop-motion clay model of my penis. Filming that one was hilarious and awkward in equal measure.[7]

Most of these videos were available on YouTube until I did BGT when it was suggested that some of them may be a little too personal so I took them all down. Maybe they will be back up by the

---

[7] I was due to perform on another luxury line, a competitor of Silverseas; Seabourn. Same luxury, same small ships, same butler service. I was going to be away for two weeks, long enough to film a three minute stop motion video. I took flesh coloured clay and modelling tools in my hand luggage and proceeded to create a small film studio in my suite. I had my camera on a tripod and a small light pointing at a desk chair on which I'd stuffed a pillow from the bed into the top of a pair of my jeans. Poking out of the jean's zip was the model of an erect clay penis complete with eyes and mouth on the helmet area. It took most of the first day to set everything up and then I went for dinner. When I returned later after copious complimentary wine and one of the best fillet mignons I had ever tasted, my bed had been turned down, fresh towels were on the rail, a chocolate was placed carefully on my pillow and my small studio remained untouched. I started giggling to myself when I imagined what my stewardess must have been thinking when confronted with that scenario.

I've drunk in many crew bars over the years and heard incredible stories from stewardesses about walking in on couples copulating, gentlemen enjoying some 'alone time' and all manner of other scenarios but I bet they hadn't seen this one before. I made a note to meet my stewardess at the earliest opportunity and explain everything but that earliest opportunity never came! I kid you not. They are so good on these vessels at knowing exactly when you've left your room to dash in and do what they need to do before you return. They're the ninjas of the housekeeping world and in two weeks, I never met her. I thought about leaving a note to explain but the longer it went on, the funnier it became and I just presumed that eventually, we'd run into each other but we never did.

time you read this. One of them made it into my first tour. I'd written The Love Story Of Lego and made another stop motion video to accompany it in 2017. This is when I was spending weeks away on cruise ships and had a lot of free time. When I was putting my tour show together in 2021, the creative team I was working with asked if I had any other original songs and Emmah suggested I play them the Lego Song. I didn't think it would work outside of our family unit but my team didn't agree. They loved it and the video that went with it, and sure enough, it got a great response from audiences around the country. I introduced it as a nod to any children in the audience even though the moral of the whole song wasn't exactly child-friendly.

The Love Story Of Lego

I wish I was a Lego figure, being a Lego figure rocks
Play with me for hours and hours let me stay in your Lego box
I wish I was a Lego figure with interchangeable legs and tops
Only one store I'd have to shop in, buy my outfits in Lego shops.

So play with me indefinitely and we will be the love story of Lego.

I wish I was a Lego figure with shiny plastic yellow skin
And although I'd have no fingers everything would just fit in
I wish I was a Lego figure if I felt sad for just a while
I'd change my head and find another and give myself an instant smile

I'd drink wine and not fall down
Spin my head to look around
But it could be a lonely life
You'd have to be my Lego Wife
Then we could both be Lego figures

Walking through a Lego land
Doing Lego things together
Wishing we could hold Lego hands.

We could be a Lego family with two little Lego boys
Easier to reprimand them when your kids are Lego toys
If Alfie punches Nathan simply pull off both of Alfie's hands
And when Nathan starts his whining pull his head off where he stands
No need for any babysitters, we could go out sitter free
Just disassemble them entirely, how much trouble could they be?

But you don't see many Lego babies, are Lego figures all monastic?
Or do we deduce they can't reproduce
Because their reproductive organs are made of plastic?
Would I still be romantic and wine and dine ya
With no penis or plastic vagina? (Actually, I think you can buy them)

So on second thoughts let's not be Lego, flesh is better any day
Leave the Lego to the children, come upstairs with me to play
Come play with me indefinitely and we will be a love story
And I will just be Jon,
And although Lego's fun
And the image of your bum
Is always quite fantastic
If it was in a Lego thong
For kids it might be wrong
But it inspired this song
I'm glad it's not yellow or made of plastic.

So I had a plan for the Royal Variety Show; all of Emmah's previous Christmas songs had been composed and recorded while I was away on the ships, so by November 2020 I just hadn't had the opportunity to write one for her having been at home since March and being a little preoccupied. I'd explained as much and she completely understood. Thirteen was a good number to stop at and it was thirteen more songs than most people had been given as Christmas presents so I felt OK about the tradition coming to a natural end.

Then I imagined writing her a song and revealing it on television, on stage, on the show. It was due to be broadcast on 27th November so close enough to Christmas to warrant a few sleigh bells. That would be the way to end the tradition surely? I wrote 'Cosmos At Christmas' and made a rough edit of some VT that could play behind me as I was performing it knowing from my experience on BGT that they would have editors to polish my ideas and everything would need to go through clearance anyway.

Now the more alert reader at this point may be yelling at their book that I have lied. That I could have potentially misled you or indeed led you up the garden path (make your mind up). What happened to the song idea I had the morning of the BGT finals that I revealed to Ant and Dec after I had been announced as the winner? Was that a fabrication? Did I lie to the great British viewing public, 35% of whom had given me their votes and their goodwill on the understanding that I would never seek to do anything with them up a garden path? Am I a LIAR???

Calm down and stop shouting at your book. People are staring. What I had dreamt of, or thought of through sleep-encrusted eyes was an introductory verse that would precede whatever song I was going to compose for the show. It was a nod to those that had gone before me. A small musical tribute to those giants I spoke of earlier, all of whom I had watched on the Royal Variety Show or the Palladium stage when I was younger. But the issue here is one of editing. I did perform that verse on the show before singing 'Cosmos At Christmas' but it was edited out for the broadcast. This is common practice as the show runs for well over two hours but only has a 90-minute slot in the television schedule. Lots of acts are edited. Jason Manford, the host of the show in 2021, spoke to me about it after it had been broadcast and I was feeling a bit pissed off that they'd cut my opening verse, especially as I was scheduled to be a part of a Les Dawson documentary that year and had told them that he was part of my tribute on the show. Jason had agreed with the producers that he could be there for the editing process knowing that some of his material was going to be cut and wanting to make sure none of the edits ruined any of the jokes. Ah, the joy of experience. For the record, the lyrics, almost as I had dreamt them the morning of the finals show were:

> There have been so many famous pianists on this show,
> All superstar celebrities, all people that you know:
> Jerry Lee's Great Balls Of Fire burned here long ago,
> From the flamboyance of Liberace to the songs of Manilow.
> Not forgetting dear Les Dawson, who nearly broke the piano.
> And now you're sat there wondering eagerly
> Who's following in the footsteps of those legends?
> Well, it's me.

On one of our production Zoom calls, the producers of the show seemed very impressed that I already had the song written. Not every winner of BGT going back to 2007 had been quite as prepared. What was to follow this dreamt-of introductory verse was a quirky love song about getting pissed at Christmas and likening my Wife to a Muppet:

Cosmos At Christmas

Like Laurel and Hardy, Barker and Corbett,
Eric and Ernie, Bernie and Snorbitz
Sooty and Sweep, Bombastic and Shaggy,
I'll be your Kermit, if you'll be Miss Piggy.
If I'm Danny from Grease, I may not be as cool,
But you weren't as innocent as Sandy at school.
Like Oceans and cruise ships, canals and barges,
You're my Ryan Air, I'm your hidden charges.

We'll have cosmos at Christmas, and pornstar martinis,
Christmas morning: bellinis
We'll toast our loved ones and we'll look around us
At the smiles on our boys and the joys that are Christmas.

We go together like
Del Boy and Rodney, like Stephen Fry and clever
Like bunnies at Easter, like chocolate… whenever,
I love you as much as you love your TV,
Celebrities in jungles, Husbands on BGT.

More than Boris loves Donald,
More than Micky loves Minnie,
More than Beckham loves football,
More than Posh loves being skinny,
More than Sinatra and swing, tantric and Sting,
The crown jewels and bling,

So I'm gonna sing:

We'll have cosmos at Christmas, and pornstar martinis.
Christmas morning: me and you with bellinis.
We'll toast our loved ones and we'll look around us
At the smiles on our boys and the joys that are Christmas.

And even though everything one day comes to an end,
Like the last page of a good book or the last series of Friends,
So our kids will grow older and leave their father and mother
But we'll survive that chapter too because we'll have each other.

And we'll have Cosmos at Christmas, and pornstar martinis.
Sushi and oysters, baby that's you and me,
We'll toast our loved ones and we'll look around us
At the joy and the love that's not just for Christmas.

Chapter 13
More Delays & Diazepam

On October 17th, feeling rough with Covid and even sicker with worry, I was scheduled to do an interview via Zoom with BBC News. I've watched it back a few times now and can't fathom what was going on. I got myself out of bed, splashed cold water on my face, even brushed a little bronzer on to try and hide my pale, poorly complexion and settled in front of my camera ready for the interview. It started innocently enough with questions about the show, how it felt to win and how proud my family were, and then they asked how I was feeling. I thought I'd done a good job of hiding my covid-ness so I was a little taken aback. I hadn't posted anything on social media about being ill, I'm not sure why. People were dropping like flies with this damn virus and many were sharing their recovery on various platforms but I guess I decided that if we weren't advertising the cancer situation then we may as well keep quiet about the 'Rona too.

"I'm fine, thank you," I answered not managing to hide my intrigue about what they were implying because they continued:

"You haven't been well we heard. Everything OK?"
Again, slightly hesitantly but calling on all my improv and acting skills so far kept well hidden from the public along with my health I replied:

"Well I was feeling a little run down immediately after the show but I guess that was to be expected. It was quite an intense few days but no, I'm fine. Thanks for asking."

For a fleeting moment, the hosts looked slightly confused and there was a long enough pause for me to know that they had been prepped to try and get an exclusive. Despite our best efforts to keep everything quiet, something had been leaked but even the media has to follow some sort of guidelines and as I'd learnt after my early hospital visit, they weren't allowed to report on anything medical without my permission so they were trying to get it from the source. We all stared at each other for what seemed an age but in fact, was barely a second and the rest of the interview went ok.

Emmah joined me in the lounge afterwards having been on her best behaviour ever since her This Morning camera bomb and agreed that it had been a weird moment. She didn't think anyone else would have picked up on it and she thought that I'd covered it well considering I was breaking out in a cold sweat from the virus anyway. I crawled back into bed and drifted back to sleep wondering if the whole interview had just been a ploy to pursue whatever lead they'd been given. But then I'm also a sucker for the most far-fetched conspiracy theories so pay no attention.

I was bedridden for five days but tested negative on the sixth so contacted the hospital who explained their additional quarantine policy of an extra week after the NHS's recommended ten days. Every bit of news that delayed my operation hit me like a mental brick in the face. Nights got shorter as I found it harder to drop off but was still waking up far too early. Meetings in the bath with General Diazepam and Sergeant Single Malt were a sporadic, temporary, welcome relief and I was enjoying revisiting West Wing on my phone as I concentrated on keeping my face out of the water, but the anxiety and fear always came flooding back as soon as my defence cloud evaporated and no amount of self-reasoning seemed to alleviate it. My biggest fear at the time other than actually having cancer was that this was changing who I was on a molecular level. God that sounds wanky even as I type it. What I mean is, I've always been generally happy. Someone who you'd describe as optimistic although I think we all flit between extremes depending on what life throws at us. I think my friends would describe me as pretty upbeat. Probably more of a natural introvert, those that know me well, who's able to turn it on when he needs to but is quite happy sat with a book and his own company. I was the guy that would try and make you smile if you were down rather than want to wallow there with you but this experience felt like it was sapping me of all my optimism. I was now the guy that needed cheering up and I have so rarely been that in the past. It felt like my diagnosis or even just my potential diagnosis was altering the core of who I was and it scared me to think I might not come back from it.

I was also very disappointed in myself for not handling it better. I was neither brave nor strong. I wasn't 'battling' as so many people are said to do, I was almost just lying down and admitting defeat and I hadn't even been told anything definitive at this point. It was also around this time that BGT phoned to say that the Christmas Show was back on… I was going to need another song for some serious prime-time telly so thankfully that gave me something to focus on.

My seventeen-day quarantine ended on 9th November and they must have been keen to get under my skin as I was booked in that day for my third Covid test. Assuming that it was going to be negative they also booked me in the next day for the radioactive isotope injection that I needed twenty-four hours before my op. They did explain the reasons why but I can't remember them and it's not important. I was back the next day and glowing with radiation when my consultant came to find me to break the news that I was still testing positive!!! I think I shed a tear. It was getting too much. It meant my next test might clash with the Royal Variety show and if I was isolating then I wouldn't be able to do it at all. I pleaded my case with the hospital. I had no symptoms and hadn't had them for weeks. Surely cancer posed a bigger threat to me than Covid. My consultant went to the board of surgeons and they agreed that the cancer was potentially more harmful than Corona but policy was policy and I would have to wait.

My fourth test was scheduled for 30th November which at least left me clear to do the show but then I wondered if that was a good idea anyway. What if I contracted a new case while I was around all those people despite masks and distancing protocols? Was it too much of a risk? All this just mashed my head on top of the anxiety that was becoming quite debilitating at times.

Doubting their testing kits, I booked myself in for a drive-thru NHS test the next day but that too was positive so I did what I had avoided doing ever since my mole had been diagnosed and I turned to Google. Not for the mole, oh no. There's no way I was typing 'malignant mole' into Google. You can type in the symptoms of the common cold and be told you're going to die of the Black Death so that wasn't going to happen but t'internet did offer up a lot of information about false positives. Apparently, some cells are effectively dead and they can remain in your nose long after you are asymptomatic so you can still test positive on a swab and they can remain there for months! Extensive research had been carried out in South Korea but frustratingly the UK and in particular Christie's was paying it no heed.

I tried to distract myself by getting the carpet fitted in the new studio (we were still calling it the garage, that would have to stop) and writing a new song for the Christmas show and also the new songs I was writing for Neil Jones' tour, Gingerland. Neil is one of the professional dancers on Strictly, the ginger one if you're trying to visualise him, hence the name of his tour. Neil had gotten in touch just after my audition had been broadcast telling me he thought we shared a sense of humour and would I be interested in writing the opening song for his show. He gave me a brief synopsis and I came up with a Barry White-type soul number which I was quite pleased with. So was Neil apparently as he suggested I write the whole show! The next brief was a Viennese Waltz between two Gingerbread people. I came up with a ridiculous lyric to a lush string-laden waltz and he loved that too. We agreed that he'd discuss details with his producers but we'd be looking at an album of the show and we chatted more about expanding the storyline and other musical numbers. Look at me writing a musical![8]

On top of that, I was also performing a lot of virtual shows. These were the gigs that I would have been driving up and down the motorways for if I had won the show in normal circumstances so although performing to just a camera lens, sometimes with absolutely no audio from the audience, was far from ideal, I was definitely getting better at it and I could even perform a show in my slippers. Small win.

Doing comedy to a silent lens is horrible but I was lucky that I had the piano to accompany me, not just for the songs but as a timing aid when I was talking to my invisible audience. I could use the pauses where you can only hope your viewers are laughing to tinkle a few notes before moving on. It must have been working because the feedback that I was getting from my management company was fantastic. I just wasn't getting it during the actual shows. A post-it note stuck directly beneath the lens of my camera said it all: 'Remember the audience IS there!'

Of course, most of these companies were also requesting bespoke songs which at times pushed my creative limits. I'd created a form for Jo Allen to send to bookers to help with the content of these new compositions. They all wanted something funny and uplifting, helping their employees to see the light at the end of the

---

[8] Unfortunately, this was to be another casualty of Covid and the tour got cancelled in 2021 which weirdly I found out about on Twitter. I'm waiting for another opportunity to use the Gingerbread dance song but I think it may be a little niche.

Covid tunnel while making them laugh at my lyrical genius in capturing the essence of their jobs and businesses. More often than not I'd be supplied with the company's name, a list of their senior workforce and the company's mantra or objectives. Maybe a few statistics if I was lucky. It was painful trying to create something that I was happy to put my name to but as Emmah would continually remind me, my worst effort would probably be better than their best so I should stop trying to write the next earworm to worry Ed Sheeran and just try and make their company name rhyme with something topical and maybe take the piss out of the CEO.

One request came from a company that ran several veterinary surgeries. I would be opening their annual conference, albeit virtually. They wanted a twenty-minute show to include a bespoke song. I came up with the cute idea of having it sung by a dog. Not literally you understand, that would have taken more training than I had time for, just sung from the perspective of a dog. I wrote some lyrics that I felt were much cleverer than some of my other corporate efforts, this could even stand alone as a little comedic ditty if I removed the name of the company and made it more generic. The dog was singing about how much he didn't like going to the vet because every time he went, they shoved a thermometer up his arse or shaved a bit of his fur off or forced a pill down his throat. One time he fell asleep there and when he woke up his balls were gone. The song's tagline was the dog saying that if he did have to go to the vet then it had better be one owned by this company because they were lovely and he enjoyed going there because they were kind to animals and made him feel calm. Pretty straightforward you'd think.

I recorded the song with a fun, uptempo accompaniment and sent it off as most of these companies wanted a preview. Sometimes that was beneficial to me if I'd got a bit of information slightly incorrect or misspelt an acronym or two but I thought this one was in the bag.

They hated it. No way did they want a song that was criticising vets. How dare I suggest that they stuck thermometers up arses or castrated poor defenceless pups and pussies?! They didn't say that last bit but that was the gist of it. I despaired, rewrote it and took the cheque. It does remind me though to look at that one again and see if there's something I can use in my regular show.

Around this time I decided I had to do the Royal Variety Performance no matter what. Part of my argument to myself, perhaps dulled by Diazepam, was if the cancer was going to get me, I'd better tick off a bucket list while I still had the opportunity.
I told you I was going to some dark places.

Chapter 14
The No-Royal, No-Audience, Variety Performance
Part 2

I was having regular chats with the show producers. My little song was being orchestrated so I would be accompanied by the thirty musicians on stage and I managed to persuade them that the military drummers would be a good idea too. I got back in touch with my old school.

The idea to use them, originally in the finals of the show, had come from Simon Marsh the head of music at RHS (That's The Royal Hospital School as opposed to The Royal Horticultural Society. I'm not sure they even have a music department.) Simon had messaged me not long after my audition had been broadcast offering the services of the marching band should I think of any opportunity where they could contribute something. Once I'd written Small Things I felt the uplifting, patriotic tone of the ending would benefit from some military snare drums but as we know, that wasn't to be. Now I'd written Cosmos At Christmas which didn't have a segment for drummers at all but then I had the idea of doing a short reprise of Small Things as the climax to my performance as the ending of 'Cosmos' was quite downbeat. An hour in the studio gave me the segue between the two numbers and I emailed Simon with my idea who was immediately on board, even after I'd explained there'd be no Royal Family, or indeed no live audience. It was still a great opportunity for his young musicians, he just had to sell the idea to the Headmaster.

I ran it by the producers who loved the idea. I initially went for the full drum corps of about twelve drummers but this gradually got reduced to just four, allowing for dressing room space and more bloody social distancing rules. I let Simon decide who the four lucky winners were and we began rehearsals via video messages and emails.

Headlining the show would be Michael Ball who was singing a duet with Sir Captain Tom on a video link, Gary Barlow who had a new single to promote, Mel C from the Spice Girls and Steps. That would be interesting. Long before Steps had been formed I'd worked at a Warner's Hotel with Faye (she's the tall, blonde one) and we'd dated for a few months. I'd performed a show at an event for her parents and had managed to smash her Dad's car door against their driveway gate when I'd offered to help her park it. She had also been my assistant in a comedy routine that I performed with a magic illusion called the substitution trunk. I'd had a very lifelike old-lady mask made out of latex which Faye wore along with an old lady coat as she walked through the audience during my show. I'd invite her to help me with a trick and perched her on the edge of the trunk before accidentally knocking her inside it. The audience were convinced I'd just potentially killed an elderly member of the audience. Then there was a bit of business which resulted in me locking the trunk, standing on top and us switching places instantly behind a large curtain. Faye was revealed standing on top of the box in the traditional magician's assistant costume of leotard and sequins and I was released from inside the trunk. We hadn't really been in touch since she'd left the hotel and subsequently auditioned for Steps.

Years later I was in a coffee shop with my mate Andy flicking through the latest edition of the lad's mag FHM who were promoting their 100 sexiest women in the UK. Faye was number 11 and I could not convince Andy that we'd once been an item. Not sure he even believes me to this day. I was pretty chuffed though. I really am that shallow.

On the drive to Blackpool for rehearsals my manger called me and asked if I minded her passing my number on to Jason Manford who had asked if he could call me. Jason is a great comic and TV presenter who had appeared on the RVP three times before as an act but this would be his first time hosting. I assumed it was a courtesy call to the new bloke to wish me good luck and was thinking how thoughtful of him when he called me.

"Hi Jon. It's Jason."

"Hello mate. Really kind of you to call."

"Not at all. Looking forward to working with you. Listen, you know this is going to be done without an audience right?"

"Yeah. Not ideal is it."

"It's a bloody nightmare. They've installed about 200 monitor screens in the stalls section of the theatre with different people on every screen watching the show on a live stream."

"Wow," I offered, "That's an improvement on a giant wall with a thousand people on a Zoom call at least."

"Well that's why I'm calling pal. You're the only person I know who's performed to a virtual audience on that scale. Got any tips for me?"

I started laughing. There was me thinking he was phoning to offer me some advice and wish me good luck and now he was asking for my help. I was going to disappoint him:

"Jason, I only had to perform for three minutes at a time. You've got to hold it together for over 2 hours. I think you're on your own pal!"

I was apologetic but told him I'd be there in the wings cheering him on if it helped. The only advice I could offer was to ask the sound engineer for some sort of audio feedback from the audience, even if it was faked. We both knew that applause and laughter could be added in post-production but it would kill your timing if you couldn't hear anything after a punchline, not to mention your confidence. At least he'd have the luxury of being able to stop and start until he got it right. He was the perfect choice to host this unusual version of the show though and he nailed it.

Emmah had travelled up with me for the rehearsals day ostensibly to keep me company but I'm sure she was hoping to meet Gary Barlow. Not so much Faye. We collected our lanyards both of which now hang around my certificate of participation, in my studio and we were shown to the coffee shop in the Winter Gardens. It turns out that all the headliners weren't going to be there until the next day, it was only a few of us that were rehearsing that day but I loved having Em with me and she gave the seal of approval to my song. No, I'm afraid the first time she heard it wasn't really on the broadcast of the show. There's no way I couldn't have told her what I was going to perform. If I'd told her it was a secret she'd have probably guessed it was a song for her anyway. We met up with my school drummers and their head of music. They were pretty excited to be there and Simon couldn't stop thanking me. They looked amazing in their band uniforms and I thought it was going to a fabulous part of the show.

Two days later I was back on my own to record the actual show. It was lovely to see Faye again and I couldn't help but ask her what she'd been up to since we broke up. Before I saw her in person backstage there was a very strange moment as I was dropping my bags in my dressing room and I heard her voice on the monitor which relays the audio from the stage. She was talking about not wanting to go into the box or something. I wandered into the wings and watched her rehearsing a magic trick with Stephen Mulhern where he was putting her inside a box and squashing her. So she hadn't come that far really.

Before we started to record the show we needed to rehearse the finale song with the whole cast on stage. I thought as the new boy that was there because I'd won a competition, that I'd be towards the back where the fabulous NHS choir were lined up but I was stood in the second row just between Jason and Michael Ball. I'd never met Michael but we had a lot of mutual friends so I was excited to say hello when he turned around, noticed me and exclaimed:

"Jon Courtenay! I bloody love you!"

In reply, I just managed to point and tell him what his own name was:

"You're Michael Ball!"

So that was nice. We sort of made an informal arrangement that I would be a guest on his BBC Radio 2 Sunday show sometime in the future. (I was and it was virtual of course. Michael's producer asked if I could write a song and I came up with a sycophantic composition about how much of a fan I was. It's on YouTube. I got a phone call in the middle of rehearsals for the BGT Christmas show and ten minutes notice that I was going to be live on air. One of the producers at BGT rushed me to a small room backstage at the Hammersmith Apollo that would be quiet but the signal was terrible so I did the whole interview standing on a chair holding my phone near the window. What a pro.)

I never did feel like I was only there because I'd won a competition, everyone made me feel very welcome. There was a surreal moment when Gary Barlow and Mel C were on either side of me and we were chatting. I tried to hold it together but ended up waffling something about Take That and The Spice Girls being the soundtrack to my young, adult life and here I was… blah blah blah. They didn't seem to be as impressed as I was despite both of them chatting to the longest-reigning champion of BGT. To be fair at that point they wouldn't have known that I *was* the longest-reigning champion as the announcement of the cancellation of BGT for 2021 hadn't been made yet so I'll let them off for being so blasé.

It was another very strange theatre experience thanks to Covid with all the television monitors in the seats downstairs while a lot of cameras filled the rest of the space with a giant autocue monitor at the back. I'd been asked if I wanted to use it for the lyrics to my song and I jumped at the opportunity. Even though this time I would be able to stop if I forgot any words I didn't want to risk it. I'd also had to send the producers a script of any chat I wanted to say so they'd put this on the autocue as well which was a little weird. I wanted to ignore it so I came across as more relaxed and spontaneous but when it's fifteen feet across right in your eye line it's difficult to not read it, especially as I'd been told my main camera was just below it. Even with the words scrolling in front of me, I managed to mess up and substitute 'dishwasher' for 'washing machine' which made no sense in the joke I was trying to tell. It didn't matter as it was all cut out of the broadcast anyway along with my opening tribute verse. They did send me a copy of the recording with my full performance intact but made me swear that I would never post it online so instead I recorded the missing bits in my studio with the RVP logo on my green screen and that's available to see on my YouTube channel if you fancy it.

Another cancelled after-party thanks to you-know-what meant that everyone was just expected to drive home after the show and that was tough. A big anti-climax but at least I wasn't buzzing from meeting the Royal Family so thank goodness for that. (!) However, It did result in a very generous gesture from the Chairman of the charity when they announced the tickets for the 2021 show were going on sale plus the opportunity to buy tickets to the after-party and I got an email with the details. The show was to be at The Albert Hall and tickets were expensive... I think a box on the grand tier was £7,500 with an extra £130 for the party afterwards. I sent a light-hearted text saying they were rubbing my nose in it and immediately got a reply saying they would send tickets for the show and the party for me and Emmah to attend. If you don't ask...

It did result in a very funny photo though. I'd bought a new suit not long before the 2021 show to wear for a performance I was doing as part of Comic Relief. It was black with small red, metallic spots all over it to symbolise red noses. Emmah and I had great seats for the show, I was next to Sir Captain Tom's daughter who thanked me for giving him a name check in Small Things and Ed Sheehan was one of the big names on the bill. You know that guy who's worth about £200 million? It was quite refreshing to see him walk out on stage in the same suit that I was wearing: £200 from an online shop! I was looking forward to seeing him at the after-party and getting a photo taken with him but apparently, he was mortified that we were wearing the same outfit so he never showed up. (I have no idea if that's the reason he didn't come but I'm going with it.) Instead, I found a photo of him online when he was backstage meeting Prince William after the show so I shared it next to a photo of me wearing my suit. I swear it was as simple as that, no Photoshopping. It was only after a few comments that I looked at the photo and realised if you glanced at it quickly, Ed's out-stretched arm to shake William's hand looked as if he was about to shake hands with me. A lot of people presumed that he was and that we'd been hanging out and I hate disappointing people so I kept quiet.

So although 2020 was a very different Royal Variety experience to most years, I'm very thankful for a few things: That it still went ahead at all, that it didn't clash with my operation date, that I didn't catch Covid while I was there and that I'm now part of the history of the show that I grew up watching with my Mum and Dad. I just wish Dad could have seen it.

Chapter 15
Skin Graft

Emma (no h) had explained to my surgeon weeks earlier what my career was and that I was on the TV. Because he didn't watch TV or even own one, he had no scale of fame to relate to and immediately assumed I was as famous and successful as any A-lister. During our first conversation, I had tried to explain that I wasn't Ricky Gervais-famous or Ant & Dec-recognisable but he either didn't understand or just chose to ignore me and I'm sort of glad it worked out that way because he'd decided I would be a worthy recipient of a new man-made sub-dermal skin substitute trial. It had never been used at The Christie before and the manufacturers had asked my consultant if he would like to do the trial. As I was a 'very famous person on the telly' would it be in my interests to not have an unsightly dent in the side of my head? I said even if I wasn't famous or on the telly I would rather not have a dent in the side of my head. This new product reduced the disfigurement to almost nothing although I was warned (with a straight face) that I would be unable to grow hair in that area. Not really a deal breaker for me. I gratefully accepted and decided I wouldn't try and play down my celebrity ever again.

In the weeks following my BGT win, I was sent all kinds of things for free, from cupcakes to posters to boxes of sweets. At first, I didn't get it but it was explained to me that while they were no doubt being very generous and celebratory, they would also be hoping that I would post a photo of me with their presents on my social media pages. Of course. And that's generally why celebrities get free shit. The bigger the celebrity, the bigger the social media following so the bigger the amount of free shit. A quick Google search reveals the kind of money that celebrities a little higher up the alphabetical list than me can get paid for an Instagram post. (That would be A-listers rather than C-listers which I'm only on because of my name. Obvs.) Dwayne 'The Rock' Johnson with over 200 million followers can expect a company to pay him upwards of $1 million for a single post. The Kardashians are not far behind. I am very grateful to the small, independent local companies who sent me their products and I hope my tweets and posts to my thousands of followers resulted in an extra sale or two. It was my pleasure.

So, Covid test number five was on 30th November and I was negative. Insert party emojis here: [ ] I also needed to have an MRSA test done and that resulted in one of the best reactions to my new celebrity-ness. I was in a small room with just a chair, a desk and an attractive 20-something-year-old nurse who was happily chatting away with me, both of us in masks. She was going to need to do an armpit and groin swab so her chat was probably just a natural way for her to put her patients at ease. My real name is Jonathan Young so hospital records don't help if you're thinking I look a bit like Jon Courtenay, that bloke who just won a show on the telly, and you want confirmation. Also, I never assume that anyone knows who I am anyway, so this was one of my funniest fan encounters:

"Have you been busy?" she asks in a friendly, slightly enthusiastic manner.

"Yeah. It's been a bit crazy," I answer.

"Oh great. It's difficult for so many people isn't it? What do you do?"

So now I have a choice. Lie or get into the whole BGT conversation which sometimes is as short as "Oh, sorry, I don't watch that crap."

"I'm an entertainer,"

"Oh that's fab. What do you do?"

"I play piano and do comedy."

Now there's a definite pause in the conversation as she stares at my eyes for almost too long. Then she leans over to the desk and glances at my paperwork.

"Have you… are you…." she sort of stammers and trips over her words. I hesitantly confirm what I think she's intimating:

"Yeah, I won BGT last month."

Now her eyes go quite wide as she manages to replace the swab that had just been in my armpit inside its plastic tube before walking the four paces to the corner of the small room and tries to hide the small squeal that comes from behind her mask. She immediately turns back around and walks back to stand beside my chair, now obviously a little discombobulated.

"I'm so sorry. I literally watch your YouTube clips every day. You're amazing…"

She goes on for a bit saying lovely things until at the end of her fan rant she suddenly exclaims:

"Oh no… I'm meant to swab your groin now! I can't do it! Can you do it yourself?"

This is one of many interactions that makes it clear I'm very much not a sex-symbol kind of celebrity. I can't imagine she'd have had any trouble swabbing the groin of Harry Styles once she'd confirmed it was him.

The radioactive injection was on 3rd December and the operation was on 4th. I was told results would take 2-3 weeks which put Christmas Day as the last possible day I could find out if the cancer had gone any further. Thankfully I remember nothing about the operation. I woke up in the recovery room with a bright blue, round sponge measuring about 10cm across and 4cm thick stapled to my head and two rows of stitches in my neck where the sentinel lymph nodes had been removed. I was groggy but they perk you up with cups of tea and within a few hours I was dressed and Emmah was driving me home in time for me to pack. We had a train to catch the next morning to London to record the BGT Christmas show.

I'd written a song that had a vague storyline. The idea was Alfie had written a letter to Father Christmas and I'd found the letter, taken it to the piano and the words of the letter were the lyrics to the song. Ideally, I wanted to act out the story on stage with a young boy in a bed and the letter on his bedside table. I suggested that as Alfie had experience in front of the camera and as I was his Dad, he would be the ideal choice to play the part of my son and the producers had agreed. It meant that despite Covid restrictions, we would all get to travel to London together and be part of the filming as Alfie would need a chaperone for when I was busy. I'd also requested a large Santa hat to cover my blue sponge. Still not wanting the true story to become public until I knew what I was dealing with, I told them I'd just had a small operation and would need to cover the scar.

I certainly wasn't feeling at the top of my game as we sat on the train. Occasionally light-headed with a consistent dull headache it was a case of the show must go on. I was due to perform my song as the last act of the night and then stay on stage as I was accompanied by Ant and Dec plus some dancers and we'd all end the show singing I Wish It Could Be Christmas Every Day while snow machines hidden around the top of the auditorium showered us with fake snow. I was wearing a large peaked cap that I'd bought online in an XL size to cover the sponge so it was straight to wardrobe to see what hat they'd rustled up for me. It was beautiful! As luxurious as I imagined the real Santa's hat might have been if he'd enjoyed a bit of bling.Thick fur around the edge and red sequins. My operation would be hidden in plain sight.

As usual at these events, there was a lot of hanging around especially as I was the last act on. Performers were ferried from our hotel to the Hammersmith Apollo and back again to record their performances keeping us as separated as possible so I didn't really get to see many people. It was about 9pm when I got picked up with Emmah and the boys and when we got to the theatre it was obvious that it had been a long day for everyone there. The judges, Ant and Dec and all the crew had been recording non-stop for pretty much the whole day, we just had my segment and the finale to film and everyone could pack up and go home. If only it was going to be that simple.

Alfie was tucked up in bed on stage in his very fetching striped pyjamas from some time in the 1950s. His job was to be asleep which he managed with absolute professionalism. The director asked him to sit up at the end when the snow began to fall and look up in wonder but he was far too comfortable where he was, he may actually have nodded off so you didn't get to see him when it was broadcast. I had to walk into his 'bedroom', pick up the letter from his bedside table, carry it to the piano and perform the song. On the first attempt I got as far as the second verse and then just messed up a bit so apologised and asked if we could start again. On the second attempt, I messed up again and started getting a bit stressed with myself also because I knew how exhausted everybody must be. This was a song that I'd written, there was no excuse for me not being able to nail it except my head was pounding. The theatre lights were so hot and the more I worried about messing up, the harder it was to concentrate. I felt as if I'd never been on stage before and instead of it being my happy place as it had been my whole career, now I was like a duck out of water. Every person behind every camera was glaring at me (they weren't of course but I was imagining the worst), my voice was starting to crack and sweat was pouring down my head inside the Santa hat. Emmah and Nathan were in the auditorium somewhere watching and I was about to have a full-blown panic attack. I took a deep breath, apologised again to everyone there and asked if we could go once more from the top. Alan, the lovely floor manager for this show, BGT and Saturday Night Takeaway is the man who really runs the show. He cues everyone, asks for quiet and generally makes everything run like clockwork which on any of those shows is a huge responsibility. Alan suggested I just go from when I sit at the piano as they could use what they'd already filmed for the walking on bit. I was so grateful that I didn't have to stand up as I'm not sure my legs were completely functioning at this point.

I was doing my best not to communicate the state I was in but people could tell I wasn't quite right, none more so than David Walliams, who assuming that nerves were getting the better of me, stood up from his chair and gave me the most glorious pep talk assuring me that there was no pressure, they were all there for me, they all loved me. I should just relax and enjoy the moment and try not to worry etc.

I can't remember ever feeling so frustrated. Mainly because I wasn't nailing the performance as I should be, but now they also thought I was buckling under nervous pressure and while a few nerves are always good to have in any performance, mine were always very much under control. I hated the fact that anyone might think I was anything but professional and able to handle whatever was thrown at me plus now David had been so considerate, on top of everything, I was feeling quite emotional. You know when you're about to cry and someone just opens their arms to hug you and you lose it? Well, that.

On the third attempt, I got through the whole song however bad the vocals may have been and I could have stayed there all night trying to do it better but I knew that wasn't an option. As soon as I got to the end Alan was back on stage directing it to be cleared so we could set for the big finale. I stood chatting to Ant and Dec for a bit, desperate to tell them everything but keeping it quiet and just managing small talk, I think we discussed the amount of makeup that Stephen Mulhern had applied next to me at the Royal Variety Show. Then we were ready for a quick rehearsal of the last song before we recorded it.

Alan explained that Ant and Dec would come on as if I'd just finished my song, have a quick chat with me then ask if I'd stay on to accompany everyone for the big finale while they thanked everyone and I just tinkled away and on their cue launched into the chorus of I Wish It Could Be Christmas. Dancers were dancing, I was doing my best to rock out on the piano despite sweat now making its way past my hat and into my eyes while some snow was falling. The last line would be just me: "Let the bells ring out for Christmas". One rehearsal in the bag and we're ready to record it.

By now I was feeling proper shit. The adrenaline that had got me through my song was dissipating, I was soaked through with sweat, my head was pounding and I just wanted to get out of there. So annoying as it should have been such a blast. We started recording and it all went to plan until the very last line when Ant turned to me and shouted 'Take it away Jon!' I went to take a big breath in and promptly swallowed a mouthful of fake snow which was now falling so hard I could barely see anyone else on stage. They'd saved the bulk of it all for the actual recording rather than the rehearsal and now a good handful of it was in my throat. There was nothing I could do but splutter, try to cough it out and just announce to everyone that I had a mouthful of snow. Eventually, I could sing again and I did the last line, the music crescendoed, everyone cheered, clapped and yelled 'Merry Christmas'.

I caught Alan's eye and mouthed 'I'm so sorry' assuming that we'd have to do the whole thing again but to my astonishment, he thanked everyone for their incredible efforts that day and announced 'That's a wrap.' What the hell?! There's no way they could use that as the ending to this incredible variety show, even if people thought it was a joke it was a very crap one and I was sure that I looked like a complete cockwomble but the piano was already being wheeled away. Crew with brooms were shovelling snow into bin liners and cameras were being switched off. Ant and Dec thanked me but I barely heard them. I was so upset but resigned that there was nothing I could do. I would just have to rely on the editors to try and recover what they could while deriding my name for giving them so much extra work to do. I wandered down to the judge's table where Nathan was frantically getting autographs and photos from David, Alesha, Amanda and Ashley. I thanked David for his bolstering speech and then thought 'Fuck it. There's no way I want them thinking I'm that much of an amateur.' Alesha was still sitting next to David as I asked if either of them was squeamish. David said no but Alesha wasn't too sure. I didn't give her a chance to reply before I lifted my hat to show them the surgical sponge held to my head with twenty 10mm surgical staples covered in blood and sweat that had by now leaked into the hat and the white furry edge. It was Santa-nightmare stuff.

"Jesus Christ!" exclaimed David, or words to that effect.

"Oh my god!" Alesha joined in. "What happened?"

So I explained what had taken place the day before and they were naturally surprised and full of sympathy. I felt marginally better that I had a much more valid excuse for being a bit shit than just nerves.

The next few weeks were a bit of a blur of virtual shows from my studio for various company Christmas parties, some charity shows and lots of song-writing. I wrote one of my favourite songs for The Royal British Legion when they asked me to perform a ticketed event on line to help raise funds and to celebrate their centenary. I usually try to find the funny when I'm composing, but this was different. The history of this charity and what it represents was too important to try and make frivolous jokes and I found myself writing a poignant song inspired by my Grandad.

I Wish I'd Asked Him More

He was a soldier, he went to war,
Sometimes asked what he was fighting for,
But he'd tell me stories and I'd sit enthralled;
I wish I'd asked him more.
He married true love at eighteen,
For three years their love went unseen,
Though battle scared true love endured.
I wish I'd asked him more.

Stories of sixpences and shillings,
Front doors unlocked and neighbours willing.
The history you lived, the people you know,
Tell me stories before you go.

I know that you don't want to talk
About the violence and death you saw,
But your life will always be more
Than the blitz of Hitler's war.
I've read of Christmases in trenches,
Of football games and sharing lunches,
But every lesson learnt should teach us
Why gunfire was heard on beaches.
I wish that we'd sat down before;
I could have asked you more.

In your drawer at your bedside
Are the medals and ribbons, they're just beside
The poppy and pin that you wear with pride
For the legion by your side.
Now your great-grandchildren are here,
I tell them tales of the brigadier
Who for victory stood and faced his fear
And the legion he held dear.

Tell me of the years you shared
With Grandma as the perfect pair,
Devoted love and years of care,
Those final months when she was scared.
When you held her hand and let her talk,
Often making no sense at all
But you were there and at nightfall,
You held her when she called.
I wish that we'd sat down before;
I could have asked you more.

The childhood that you gave me Mum
Helped her raise her only Son,
When my life had just begun,
Because of you I'd won.
As a parent now I hope to be
The inspiration you were to me,
We're all a part of history.
I love our memories:

The jokes you'd tell when you came round,
I wish I wrote that laughter down.

I'd see Mum's look as if you'd done wrong
But still I laughed along.
The wink you'd share when you caught my eye,
The hugs you gave when you saw me cry,
Late at night the lullabies.
I never thought about goodbye.

When you were older I'd rush to see
You standing there beside the street,
Outside the shops in cold November,
The words writ large: We will remember.
I'd feel so proud to see you there,
The smartest British Legionnaire,
Speaking of your lost comrades:
For our tomorrow, they gave their today.

So children listen if you can see
The slightest opportunity
To sit upon your Granddad's knee
And listen to stories.
Grasp every moment that you can,
I guarantee Grandad or Gran
Will have so many tales in store.
I wish I'd asked mine more.

    BGT's wardrobe department was much more generous with the Santa hat than they were with the Louboutin shoes and they let me keep it. If the shoes were showing signs of a wound leaking into them then I probably could have kept them too. So at least it was Christmas and I could wear it for all my virtual performances keeping my head drama a secret for a little longer. Emmah had told me after the Christmas show recording that she had been watching it from the back of the theatre and Amanda was standing with her as she was getting changed from an earlier performance. When you watch the show back and see Amanda sitting there watching me, that's all editing. As is the fact that I don't look completely shit. Another public thank you to the wonderful men and women who stitch the endless hours of footage together and make it look so much better than it often is. When I messed up the second time Amanda turned to Emmah and the look of sympathy on her face was enough for Emmah to tell her everything after asking her to keep it to herself which of course she did. Amanda also followed up with some messages to check how I was doing in the months to come which was very sweet of her.

A lovely moment happened when Amanda and Emmah were chatting and Nathan was also there. It all got a bit too overwhelming for him and he turned to his Mum and said:

"I can't believe you're just standing there chatting to Amanda Holden."

"What do you mean?" she asked.

"Well, she's like a huge star and you're just chatting to her like she's normal!"

Amanda was the first to interject and assure Nathan she was very normal. I think her words were: "Fuck that, I'm not a star. I'm just normal." Which she is. And very lovely.

Another song I was frantically trying to finish around this time was the opening number for the ITV pantomime. They'd asked for plenty of cheese and that I could do. I was scheduled to travel down to London to film at a piano singing the song right in front of Television Centre with some dancers and Alison Hammond as the Fairy Godmother. The Santa hat was washed and ready and it was a really fun afternoon, although it was so cold it was just as well that my piano part had already been recorded and I was just miming. There's no way my fingers were going to function in those temperatures. Covid restrictions also meant that no unnecessary visitors were allowed inside the studios and as all our segment was being filmed outside we were considered unnecessary. Charming. My dressing room was the toilet in the cafe across from the entrance along with the dancers. Don't let anyone try and convince you that showbiz is all glamour and red carpets. Sometimes it's kneeling in a toilet cubicle to do up your laces, getting a stranger's piss on your new suit trousers before being filmed wearing them and broadcast to a couple of million people.

By December 21st I still hadn't heard from the hospital despite chasing them up a few times but today there was news. My results were in… but no one had looked at them yet, could they call me back?

Yes. Yes please. As soon as you could would be lovely. If someone could just take a glance and let me know that would be delightful. Or not. Thank you so much.

No one had called by bedtime.

9am on the 22nd and I called again. Still no one had looked and now I was a bit too emotional to be polite. I explained the situation and the receptionist promised me, possibly a pinky promise, that someone would call me back the same day. Emmah had nipped out to get a bit of shopping and as she walked back into the house in the afternoon my phone rang with the familiar 'No Caller ID' that suggested it was either the hospital or someone telling me I was due PPI. We walked into the studio together now definitely no longer a garage, as I answered the phone.

Emmah and I sat on the sofa. I don't remember any of the conversation at all except the words:

"Your results are all clear. The cancer was confined to the mole." Just as well I was sitting as my knees would have buckled as I just crumpled. All of me just crumpled. From my toes to my stapled sponge. I don't remember hanging up the phone but I do remember not being able to stop crying. Every sleepless night, every early morning, every hot bath, whiskey and drug that had tried to suppress how I was feeling crumpled with me and I sobbed uncontrollably. Emmah hugged me and just let me get it all out. Then she took a photo of me (it's in the book.) It was quite a moment. We were going to have the most amazing Christmas.

Chapter 16
A New Year

It was a great Christmas, despite Covid still being a huge part of everyone's lives, it was never going to dampen the relief and joy that was bouncing off the walls in our home. I got in touch with Macmillan and explained what I'd been through and that I'd like to try and raise awareness if they could give me some advice on where to start. They were very enthusiastic as they explained how cancer was becoming 'the forgotten C' during Covid. Fewer people were going to their GPs to get suspicious lumps and moles checked out because they thought their doctor's surgeries and the NHS were too overwhelmed. I read that breast cancer cases detected through screening fell by 44% in 2020. Not because they didn't exist but because people weren't getting checked. Macmillan suggested I write a short song to promote awareness and encourage people to still get checked out. This Morning and BBC News got on board as well as The Sun newspaper and I came up with a jaunty little uptempo ditty about skin cancer. No mean feat. BBC News did cut out the 'boobs and balls' reference and that made me laugh. They consider their viewers too sensitive for such suggestions. As if it was still the 1950s. Standards are alive and well within the British Broadcasting Corporation.

The response to my little ditty was quite overwhelming and very humbling. It was so surprising to me how big my platform had become since BGT and how many people I could reach. If only I was better at social media. I'm just a typical Dad who used to post photos of his food and kids and now I am being told how important hashtags are and the optimal time to post according to my dashboard. Still goes right over my head. I even had a day of intense Instagram training which was a real eye-opener. I began to realise why some people charged so much money to do it for you and for a while they did it for me when we were trying to push ticket sales for my tour in 2021. It was one of the few times that I became aware of the disadvantage of winning the show during a pandemic, and only then because it was explained to me by my tour promoter. They had worked with previous winners and finalists from the show and knew that on average, within a month of winning the show and your tour being announced you could expect to sell up to 60% of all your tickets. Within a month of my win and by quite a large percentage of the votes, I'd only sold 6%. It was quite disheartening. So I was paying someone £600 a month to post the content that I still had to make! They'd phone me up and say things like:

"Right, it's International Women's Day next week. We need to know who the important women are in your life and we need some photos of them."

Then they'd post them with all the correct hashtags at the correct time. It seemed that I could learn to do that myself and save an extra mortgage payment every month. It was like learning a whole new business which of course it can be. Just look at the money that the top YouTubers make; millions. Lots of twenty-somethings with Ferraris and Lamborghinis in the garages of their mansions making content that just fries my brain but is as addictive as crack to my ten-year-old son who consistently asks why we can't live in a house like that where you can play Nerf wars and hide undiscovered for days. I was never going to get there when it took me twenty minutes to just type my hashtags.[9] I was getting lots of private messages on my different accounts from strangers saying thank you, that they'd heard my song on the radio or TV and had gone to get a mole checked out and their doctor had recommended they have it removed. One particular message was from a surgeon about six weeks after I had started the campaign:

> Hi Jon. You don't know me but I have a patient who came to see me with a mole that they were concerned about and I removed it only for the biopsy to show that it was a melanoma but we caught it in time. They mentioned they had heard your song and that motivated them to contact their GP. I thought you'd like to know that quite possibly you saved someone's life.

I was in bits. It was madness that a song that took less than an hour to write had achieved that. It brought it home to me what a difference you can make when you have a soapbox to stand on and how unimportant all the other frivolous stuff is. It's where social media can be a force for good instead of dragging you down the rabbit hole when you really should be doing more important things. Although who's to say that my song wasn't at the bottom of some rabbit hole and that's where it was found by the mole patient?

---

[9] I remember when the only time you used a hashtag was to play noughts and crosses and back then I had no idea it was called a hashtag. Can you even remember using the @ symbol before email or what it's actually called? Its proper name is an ampersat and a hashtag is actually called an octothorpe. Any of you compiling pub quizzes, there you go.

I've resigned myself to just being crap at social media and if I wasn't in this business I know for certain that I wouldn't even be on it. I went to see Joe Pasquale last week in his role as Frank Spencer in Some Mother's Do 'Ave 'Em. We'd worked together when I was nineteen years old and the next time we saw each other was at a charity show at the Theatre Royal in Windsor twenty-nine years later. Moments like that scare me because it really shows how quickly time flies. Chatting in his dressing room after his brilliant rendition of the hapless Frank, he told me that he wasn't on any social media and I was really quite jealous. It can be done but then Joe's had a much longer career than me in the public eye. He was crowned King of the Jungle in 2004 and he used to do the whole social media thing but got fed up with the trolls and the vitriol and decided it just wasn't healthy so stopped it all.

Like most parents, I'm very aware that my kids are growing up in a world where social media is so prevalent and there are horror stories of how badly online bullying can affect some young people with suicides not uncommon. I experienced bullying at my boarding school but the bullies had a face and only a few people were within earshot. Nowadays keyboard warriors can reach thousands of people and go unchecked when they name and shame the target of their abuse and it's not going to go away. As I mentioned earlier when I wrote Baldy With A Buzzer, I wasn't the recipient of too much online abuse but I was more concerned that people might target my eldest son Nathan. Alfie doesn't do social media yet and I hope to prolong that for as long as possible and Nathan didn't seem to attract too many nutters. Weirdly there did seem to be a few older gentlemen that tried to make contact with him but we soon quashed that.

Every parent has their techniques for raising their kids whatever books they read or advice they are given. Every child is unique and so is every parent and I think most of us are just doing our best to keep them alive until they're eighteen and we're not responsible for them any more. All we've done with both our boys is tell them we are there for them no matter what and they can talk to us about anything. You can add every parental control to your wifi and you can track every step they take but you can't protect them from every evil that is out there. Some of it will get through and you just have to hope that they'll tell you about it. So I think it's important for them to know that no matter what they've seen, done or heard, their first port of call is always Mum or Dad.

We also tell them we love them.

A lot.

Every day.

Numerous times.

Everything else is secondary.

Early February, I was sat at the piano in my studio which still smelt vaguely of fresh paint and new carpet, attempting to compose the latest corporate monstrosity that was due the next day. My left hand cradled my neck as my right hand tried to find an order of notes that hadn't been used before when I froze. In a split second, my stomach twisted into a knot as my fingers found a lump beneath them that had certainly not been there before. It was about two centimetres round and I stood to try and see in the very cool mirror hanging on the wall that I had built from the inside mechanisms of an old upright piano. (The mirror, not the wall. That was traditional brick and plaster.)

It's easy to look back on these moments knowing what happened and then dramatise it, but I can recall exactly how I felt. I had almost instantly regained my cheerful outlook on life and optimism just before Christmas, having been so scared that my experience had irrevocably changed who I was, but now it left me again like proverbial rats leaving a clichéd sinking ship and I felt despair wash over me. It started in my head and travelled through my body almost taking my legs from under me. When I say I knew, I don't mean with hindsight, I mean I KNEW that this was not just a new cyst, some little harmless bubble of fluid or fatty tissue. This was awful, unmitigated SHIT and this could NOT be happening.

Chapter 17
Tumour Two

I may have known, but it needed to be confirmed by someone other than my gut and my consultant made an appointment for me far too quickly to let me think it could be nothing to worry about. I was booked in for an ultrasound and was told that the ultrasoundologist (Google tells me that would be a sonographer) would know immediately if it was anything to worry about and if it was, he would need to remove a sample for a biopsy. Within days my neck was gelled up and pictures that appropriately looked like grey storm clouds appeared on the monitor. The sonographer commented that it was a little unclear so just to make sure he was going to inject a needle and take a sample. I called him out and relayed what I'd been told by my consultant and he admitted he didn't like the look of it.

I remember feeling quite resigned to it at that point, quite matter-of-fact. I was at my Mum's house two weeks later building a stage piano for my tour in her spare room. (The spare room was the venue for the piano-building, not the tour. That would be weird. Far too small.) I'd had this idea that I could make the shell of a grand piano out of wood and plastic and just slot a digital piano keyboard into it. It's what Elton John does although I think his shell is a real grand piano with all the innards removed so it still needs a truck to transport it. My shell was designed to fit exactly into the back of my estate car and I'd been working on it for weeks giving me a welcome distraction. After taking months to finish building it we used it once for my very first show at the Winter Gardens in Blackpool before I decided that it weighed about the same as an actual baby grand piano and took two of us well over thirty minutes to put the damn thing together. The next day I got online and bought a Dutchgrand shell made of fibre glass, imported from Belgium which can be easily lifted by one person and goes up in approximately twenty seconds. The homemade version was returned to my Mum's spare room and it was a sad day when I admitted it would never see a stage again. Then due to Mum's friend moving in as her lodger, it would need to take its final bow in our local tip. But I did thank it before I threw it away and I hope it understood that it was loved for its short life. It certainly gave me something to focus on when otherwise I would have been wallowing in self-pity.

My phone rang as I was working out how to bend the plywood frame to the curvature of one side of the piano and my consultant's secretary tried to book me in for an appointment after the weekend but I was adamant that I wasn't going to wait for the weekend and could he please call me today and tell me what I already knew. He did and I was right. A face-to-face appointment was made to discuss my options.

I can't remember what all the options were but I do remember that the one I was focussed on was not dying so the tumour was going to need to be cut out. I'd also need a full body scan to ascertain if this inconvenient cancer had found its way to anywhere else and that was going to cause an issue. The earliest date for a body scan was a week later on 1st March and the earliest date for the radical neck dissection was my Birthday, the 4th March. The problem was that the scan results could take up to a week and the operation couldn't go ahead until we had them. If they were delayed until after 4th March, the next available operation date on the NHS wouldn't be until 29th.

There are not many things in this life that I am certain of; as the saying goes it's generally just death and taxes, but let me tell you this: If you're aware that you have a cancerous tumour in your neck that somehow was aggressive enough to bypass sentinel lymph nodes and fool some of the best doctors in a hospital that deal with this sort of shit every day, you want it out as quickly as possible. Waiting around for three and a half weeks is not an option if you've recently come into some money and there is an opportunity to pay to have it done sooner.

A common question from interviewers to anyone who has won money is always 'What have you spent it on?' The same week that the money appeared in my bank account my Mum announced that she didn't want to move into the new flat that I had found for her that wouldn't require her to use stairs anymore. Mum was getting less mobile every day and I was dreading the call from a neighbour telling me she'd fallen down the stairs but she loved where she was living so the first expenditure was her stair lift. That got the expected reactions in interviews "Awww, aren't you the perfect son..." etc. which is the real reason I bought it.

One of the next purchases was something that I'm loathed to repeat here in print, as I was hesitant in telling the story in many of my shows when I was on tour but we've come this far together so here you go:

Remember the Louboutin shoes that they made me return after the finals show? Emmah announced one morning that we were going to go into Manchester and buy me a pair for my tour. I told her there was no way that I was going to spend that sort of money on a pair of shoes and she told me that I deserved it, that it would be something to mark my success with and that as I would be wearing them on tour, they would be tax deductible. (I'm making myself laugh now... that was what I said on stage, the truth is Emmah wouldn't have the first clue about tax laws, it just makes what I'm about to tell you a little more palatable.)

I agreed that we could go window shopping but I was quite happy wearing my usual white, leather Converse on stage and maybe I could buy a new pair of them for about £70. So we found ourselves in Selfridges walking towards the men's shoe section but before we got to the Converse we passed a pop-up display of shelving centred around a lush red carpet, displaying all the Christian Louboutin shoes. In the middle of one of the shelves was an incredible pair of boots covered in thousands of Swarovski crystals. The small spotlight shining on them made the light refract all around and I'm sure I heard a small choir singing 'Ahhh, ahhh, ah, ahhh' when I noticed them. They did look amazing and Emmah suggested I try them on.

Just as I was admiring my crystal-clad right foot in the mirror the salesperson waltzed over and with all the glorious camp-ness that the moment required announced:

"Oh Sir, they look fabulous on you. Just fabulous." (Lots of sibilant S's... you get the idea.)

"Yeah, they're a beautiful pair of shoes," was my nonchalant reply. Never let them know how keen you are.

"Could I ask Sir what the occasion is?" he continued. "What's the event? Anything special? A wedding perhaps?"

"Um…" I was hesitant. This was only a few weeks after I'd won the show. A few people had recognised me from my bald head or blue eyes but we were all still masked up. I had only once said out loud to someone 'I won BGT' and for some reason, it felt quite strange so I was quite enjoying being anonymous. During my time performing on the cruise ships, once you'd done your show you were a big fish in a small pond and it was a small taste of being famous. You could feel some people staring or talking about you at dinner, the all too familiar situation of being in a small elevator and standing at the front facing the doors while someone whispers behind you 'That's the guy who did the show last night' never got any less weird. Did they think I couldn't hear? Depending on my mood I'd either pretend not to, or turn round and wave hoping that their next whisper wasn't going to be 'He was a bit shit wasn't he!' That would be a long journey between floors. Generally, it was quite lovely meeting people after my shows with very flattering comments and I was always happy to stop and chat even when people would approach me in the restaurant mid-meal. It wasn't every day and it's not the worst thing in the world if someone wants to interrupt your food to tell you how much they enjoyed what you do for a living. I can imagine it might get a little tedious if you're an A-list celebrity and you can't go anywhere without being harassed but I was a way off from that level of fandom and my fragile ego always welcomed the compliments.

Not that it was always favourable. Any entertainer has stories of criticisms and complaints and I do have a favourite from back in my cruise ship days. For a while, I had a routine in my show that lasted about ten minutes only to be resolved with the most awful punchline which sort of made it funnier. It also contained a very old joke about an ex-girlfriend only having one eye. Not my proudest moment but a good 'groan' rather than a laugh. I'd performed this routine hundreds of times over the years until one show on a P&O ship when at the end of the bit a man came marching down the aisle to the front of the stage yelling at me that I was 'disgraceful' for picking on handicapped people. He then announced that his wife had only one eye and my joke had upset her so much that she had to leave the theatre. The next bit took all my willpower to remain quiet as he continued ranting:

"She's sat in the bar now, so upset. She's crying her eyes out."

Plural!!! Many of the audience nearby burst into laughter which didn't help the man's rage and he stormed out, only to walk through the door leading backstage instead of the exit. I asked the audience to calm down as in a few seconds he would have to reappear because he'd gone the wrong way. Of course, when he walked back out the entire room burst into laughter and applause. He was purple with anger.

A few months later I was back on the same ship and in my rehearsal, my band reminded me about what had happened the last time I was there. We had a bit of a giggle and that night I performed my show. Standing outside the theatre afterwards signing my CDs, I was approached by an elderly lady who had one lens in her glasses blacked out. She began by complimenting me on my show but then suggested that perhaps I shouldn't pick on people with only one eye. Now bearing in mind that in all the years of telling that joke, I had never met anyone who had been upset by it until the guy months before, so for some reason, I now presumed that this sweet little old lady was perhaps the mother of one of the band members on a family cruise deal and I was being set up. I started laughing until she went on to explain that she had contracted cancer as a child and consequently, one of her eyes had been removed. My laughing stopped abruptly as I realised that this wasn't a wind-up. What were the chances? Years of no complaints at all and then two within weeks of each other. It did make the band laugh again when I explained what had happened.

Because of Covid I still wasn't being recognised so much that it was getting uncomfortable and when I was, it was always by people who had enjoyed what I'd done. I don't know how I would have reacted to someone telling me to my face rather than just online that they thought I was crap and that the deaf choir should have won. There was one radio interview with a station broadcasting in the North West of England where the DJ told me live on air that I'd done very well even though he'd wanted Steve Royle to win because he was a mate. Not sure what he expected me to say to that.

So I hesitated before answering the shop assistant which gave Emmah time to find my winning clip on YouTube and show it to him.

"Oh my god!!!" He squealed. It may even have been the abbreviation 'OMG' but either way he was very excited, or at least he was excited on behalf of his Mum:

"My Mum loves you! She downloaded the app just to vote for you to win. This is amazing. She's going to love that I met you. Could you do a quick video on my phone for her and I can show it to her when I get back?"

"Of course," I answered graciously, "Can you discount these shoes?" He looked a little crestfallen.

"Oh I'm so sorry. We can't discount any of these I'm afraid. Even we don't get discounts for working here. I'm afraid they are £2,500."

"Sorry?" I asked.

Yeah, read that again. £2,500 for a pair of frickin' shoes. I must have stammered a reply because he continued:

"Every Swarovski crystal is glued on by hand... the leather is..."

I stopped him.

"Sorry. Stop talking. There is nothing you can tell me about these shoes that is going to make me agree that they're worth £2,500. That's just ridiculous."

I found myself actually feeling quite angry but I was still very careful when I removed them and laid them gently back on the shelf. I took his phone and walked to the corner of the store and recorded a message to his Mum. When I walked back over and handed his phone back to him, he handed me the familiar yellow Selfridge paper bag with a Louboutin box visible inside and judging by the weight it wasn't empty.

"What's going on?" I asked.

"Sir... your Wife bought them for you!" He beamed obviously quite happy with whatever sales commission he'd just chalked up. Emmah was trying to look contrite and triumphant simultaneously.

"You deserve them," she said. (I should also mention here that she'd used our joint bank account card.)

"No one 'deserves' shoes that cost that much money! Give them back, I'll buy my Converse and we'll donate £2,430 pounds to Macmillan. That is 'deserving'!"

I'd like to think that's what I said at the time but I couldn't have done the calculation that quickly. Instead, we took them home and I put the box on the shelf in my wardrobe. Almost every day I took them out to look at them to see if they looked any more valuable than the last time I'd seen them. They never did. You have a fourteen-day cooling off period to return them no questions asked provided the famous red soles didn't have a single mark on them and I kept telling Emmah that they would have to go back. She didn't agree and one afternoon when I was out she slipped her size four feet into my size eleven sparkly, immoral shoes and walked down the gravel next to our driveway.

I did make some charitable donations to try and alleviate my guilt and I did wear them on tour and I did claim them as a business expense. I also love my Wife, even when the next month in November I mentioned that as usual, I had no idea what to get her for Christmas and her casual reply was:

"Well, *you've* got a pair of Louboutins..."

I'd like to believe that it was a spontaneous thought and that it had never crossed her mind until that moment. So that's what I'll do. Because I love my Wife.

Apart from paying off a large amount of debt, we hadn't spent much more of the winnings so I found myself asking my consultant if he had an earlier appointment available in his private clinic. He did and it was the 11th of March which after a discussion with Emmah we agreed was worth the £13,000 to get this twat of a tumour removed two and a half weeks sooner. I was booked in.

If I thought I hadn't handled the first cancer news well, I was about to plummet to new depths. My newfound optimism vanished as quickly as I had regained it and my brain insisted on replaying only the worst possible scenarios most days and without fail, every night. General Diazepam and Sergeant Single Malt were reconvened but I was going to need more military might to get me through this one so Major Macmillan was contacted, this time in a professional capacity. I explained to the wonderful Nurse dealing with my case what had happened and that I needed to talk to someone who wasn't as emotionally involved as any of my family or friends. I was put in touch with a therapist and for the first time, I spoke about how I was feeling without worrying about who I was talking to. It certainly helped and my therapist made me realise the biggest emotional punch that until then had gone unacknowledged. In our first session, she asked all the questions that needed to be asked: We established that I didn't want to hurt myself and that I had no suicidal thoughts, just the opposite. I was feeling desperate because I didn't want to leave this life or my family. Like any therapist, she was keen to know how I was feeling but I couldn't articulate it very well other than 'scared' which is when she asked a question that opened the floodgates unexpectedly:

"Do you feel as if you've let your family down?"

Well, I didn't know that's how I felt but it immediately became apparent that a nail had been hit on the head as I began to sob. Even writing it now brings tears to my eyes. By ignoring that stupid little new mole over a year earlier I had been so irresponsible and because of my laziness, I could now have jeopardised the future of my family. When you're dead, you don't know you're dead, it's the people you leave behind who suffer and no parent who is trying to do their best would want any of their family to feel that way. I was devastated that it could have come to this and I was so mad at myself.

While acknowledging it gave slight relief, it didn't detract from what was going on. It was even stranger when I was asked to do a couple of interviews and they wanted to know all about my recovery and incredible 'journey' with such an upbeat, optimistic ending now that I'd gone public about the melanoma and its successful removal. I felt that going public about the latest diagnosis could detract from the positive message that I'd managed to get out there with The Mole Song so I was keeping quiet until we knew what was going on. That was tough. I listened to one of the interviews when it went out on the radio and I thought it was so obvious by the tone in my voice that all wasn't well.

Emmah and I were also keeping this from the kids. Nathan had confided after the first operation once I'd got the all clear that he'd been feeling very anxious but had kept it hidden. Every hospital visit was always just a 'checkup' and while those little white lies were easy enough, it was getting harder for me to keep the facade of my usual jovial self, especially when I was having my therapy sessions in the studio downstairs. The door would often have to remain locked for a while after the session had finished while I dried my eyes and tried to compose myself. Yet again managing to not 'battle bravely'.

I was also still trying to embrace the career opportunities that were coming my way. A lot of shows were still virtual which I was so grateful for. I'm not sure how many gigs I would have had to cancel up and down the country so I wouldn't miss hospital appointments whereas I was often performing a show to a company in London over Zoom one afternoon and then still getting to the hospital in manchester an hour after I'd finished so that was very convenient.

An exciting project that I had been working on since early February came from my 'Golden Buzzer Boys' Ant and Dec when I was asked to write the song for the End of the Show Show on Saturday Night Takeaway and perform it on the last show of the series. This was a huge deal and as usual, I'd been given a brief for the song. The producers wanted me to compose something that would cover every aspect of every episode, a roundup of all seven shows. This was going to require a lot of writing and a lot of words and the song wouldn't be able to be completed until the very last minute as so much of the broadcast is live. While it was very exciting and I always enjoy a challenge, it was going to be a lot of work but also a very welcome distraction. The first show was broadcast on 20th February and I sat down to watch it with Emmah and our boys and a pen and paper to make notes. Although my song was going to need to cover a lot of topics, we were still limited with time and it needed to be less than five minutes long. My original idea was each verse would cover an episode so I could write a bit more of the song each week but the producers had a different idea: they wanted each verse to cover a different aspect of the show as that would help with the filming. Ant and Dec wanted to perform the song with me while they relived the highlights from previous weeks. It meant that no single verse could be finished until the very last minute as we wouldn't know what was going to happen, even in the last episode that I was going to be performing in. Did I also mention that the performance was going to be broadcast live?! It was insane.

Episode two was broadcast a week later on 27th February and episode three was 6th March, by which time I was a year older and a weight off my shoulders lighter. I turned forty-eight on 4th March 2021 and was cooking a yummy lunch for Emmah and me of pan-fried sea bass with crispy leaks when I needed to Google (other search engines are available, I think) which order the breadcrumbs, flour and egg were applied to the fish. I know, ridiculous, but it's a weird thing that I have a mental block about. Typing this now, I know you apply the flour first and then the egg to make the breadcrumbs stick but every time I come to do it I second-guess myself and have to double-check. So I nipped upstairs to get my phone only to see a missed call from an unlisted caller. Knowing I wasn't due any more PPI payments my heart sank when I realised it would probably have been the hospital with the results from my body scan. I called the hotline number from the bedroom and was put through to my consultant's secretary who informed me that having checked my notes she could see that my surgeon and a senior nurse had both accessed my results earlier. I was assured that they would be notified that I had called and would no doubt call me back at their earliest opportunity.

So that was lunch out of the window. Once I'd bought Emmah up to date we pushed our fish and leeks around our plates until it went cold imagining that the senior nurse had seen my results and needed to call my surgeon. That couldn't be good. It was almost an hour before my phone rang again and Emma, the wonderful senior nurse at Christie's announced who she was and where she was calling from.

Time seemed to slow down.

I was kneeling on the carpet in my studio leaning on the small coffee table again and Emmah was standing next to me. The nurse was speaking in such a calm voice that it could only be to give bad news:

"We've looked at your scan results. Sorry we missed speaking to you earlier…"

This was becoming unbearably tense…

"…and they're all clear."

"What?!" I blurted out. Emmah's face was ashen.

"They're all clear. The tumour is just in your neck and the surgeon is confident that he can operate on it successfully."

I was silently sobbing far too hard to be able to reply to either Emma or Emmah, all I could do was give Emmah a thumbs up as she threw her arms around me and I sobbed a garbled "thank you" down the phone to Emma. She asked if I had someone with me just as my own Emmah squeezed me harder and I sobbed for a good thirty minutes.

Everything came out through those tears as we sat on the sofa in the studio again. I told Emmah the darkest places I had been to, how the anxiety had threatened to overwhelm me so many times and the sadness that I felt so deep in my soul when I imagined the worst. But as I spoke, I felt the old me returning. The optimism that I hadn't felt for so long, excitement for the future and all the things I had to look forward to came rushing back and they brought more tears. Tears of relief that I can feel welling up in me again as I write this today.

Six days later I was admitted to the private clinic at Christie's for my radical neck dissection.

Three types of neck dissection are performed when cancerous lymph nodes need to be removed. Selective neck dissection is suitable if the cancer has not spread far and fewer lymph nodes need to be removed. Muscles, nerves and blood vessels in the neck remain unaffected. Modified neck dissection is the most common with more lymph nodes being removed but nerves, blood vessels and muscles usually being unaffected. Radical is more… radical. All the tissue on the side of the neck from the jawbone to the collarbone is taken out. The muscle, nerve, salivary gland, and major blood vessels in this area are all removed. This results in some disfigurement and a list of side effects that by law I was made to listen to.

The big ones are: Stiffness of the shoulder. This is very

common and sometimes restricted movement can be permanent. It could potentially affect my ability to play the piano with my left hand. (Which as most accomplished pianists who have heard me play would tell you is quite lazy anyway. I won't bore you with details here.) Also, paralysis on one side of my face was a risk. As they would be dissecting tissue very close to my facial nerves there was a very real danger that I may be slightly lopsided. There were at least a dozen more potential issues but my reaction was always the same; it didn't matter what the dangers were, there was a very real tumour in my neck that needed to come out. While there was an option to zap it with drugs and radiation, that would never be as effective as just getting in there with a knife. Or hopefully a scalpel. You could tell me that as a result of the operation I would never be able to play the piano again, or even talk coherently, it would still be better than the alternative of not being here at all so let's just get on with it and I'll do my best to deal with the consequences.

  I was strangely matter-of-fact about it all once we had a plan in place. Typing this makes it sound like I'm boasting of bravery or something but that's not the case. I didn't feel brave, I just felt resigned. Knowing they hadn't found any more tumours was a huge relief so now we just had to get this one bad boy dealt with. It gave me hope that my anxiety and depression were just exasperated by the unknown. The worry of what could be. Now that we had a path to follow I was feeling quite optimistic about it and just wanted it done.

  Covid restrictions meant no visitors so Emmah had to drop me off at the main entrance with personal belongings to allow for up to a week in hospital. My operation was scheduled for one o'clock that afternoon and they estimated it would take about four hours. As with my previous operation, I was quite surprised by the walk to the operating table. Every operating theatre in a TV show or movie was always entered via swinging doors with the patient on a gurney and a real sense of urgency. As usual, real life is not quite as dramatic and as my surgeon pointed out, everyone in the theatre prefers it when the patient wanders in unaided!

I was half-wrapped in my gorgeous, gaping hospital gown and walked with a nurse into the operating room where I hopped up onto the table while chatting with the anaesthetist. For some reason, I decided to try and fight the drugs and was determined not to fall asleep before I reached zero on the count down from ten. I doubt I even made it to seven. I was never going to win against that cocktail of time-lapsing bliss.

Emmah called the hospital just after the four-hour mark to be told I was still in theatre. It turned out to be closer to six hours under the knife with my surgeon breaking his record of the number of lymph nodes removed. Of the six hundred lymph nodes in the body, two hundred are in the neck and I now have eighty-nine less of them on one side. I do remember coming round in the recovery room and seeing my surgeon looming over me asking me to smile before promptly falling back to sleep. It was enough of a smile to assure him that I was going to be my usual handsome self and not drooping on one side. The shoulder test would have to come later.

Three days later I was propped up in bed with two drains coming out of my neck and a self-administering morphine button next to me which I was trying not to use as I had work to do which led to an amusing situation; Episode three of Saturday Night Takeaway was broadcast on 13th March and although I had my own hospital room, unlike at home I had no way of recording the show and taking notes at my leisure. I knew Emmah would be recording it for me but I was keen to get some more of the song written so there I was with pen and notepad frantically scribbling away as my consultant knocked and came in to discuss my operation and recovery. It was an awkward moment. I was very keen to hear what he had to say and it was all quite important stuff so I didn't feel that I could ask him to come back later just because I was watching telly! But then my creative juices were flowing almost as quickly as the fluids down the tubes draining my neck and I couldn't switch either of them off. After a few minutes of quite one-sided conversation, my consultant finally had to ask:

"Am I interrupting anything?"

"I'm so sorry," I replied. "I'm writing a song to perform on this show in a couple of weeks and I have to write about what is happening on the show so I need to take notes."

"You're writing a song?"

"Well, I'm writing notes at the moment but I did start writing the song before my operation."

"And you're performing the song on television?"

"Yeah. In three weeks' time on Ant and Dec's Saturday Night Takeaway."

Two amusing revelations happened simultaneously at this point. Firstly my consultant confessed he had no idea who Ant and Dec were which is quite an achievement for anyone living in this country considering they have been a staple part of the light-entertainment scene for over twenty years.

Secondly, he became incredibly impressed:

"That's amazing. You're writing a song about a show that you're watching, to perform that song on that same show. How do you do that?"

"Say's the man who just opened me up from my ear to my collarbone and saved my life…"

He nodded thoughtfully, then added,

"I guess we all have our talents then."

"Yup. Luckily we're both quite good at what we do. But if I have a bad day, no one dies. Unless it's just me, on stage."

He didn't quite get that last reference but he smiled, nodded and said he'd come back later to discuss my physiotherapy and recovery process. I returned to the Kings of Light Entertainment, wondering what I'd missed in the last three minutes.

Chapter 18
Saturday Night Takeaway

Blog extract. 3rd April 2021

    I'm sitting in my dressing room at Television Centre waiting for the dress rehearsal to begin for tonight's End Of The Show Show on Ant & Dec's Saturday Night Takeaway. Now there's an opening sentence that I never imagined writing.

    The producer of the show got in touch with me seven weeks ago asking if I'd be up for writing a song for the final show and performing it in the studio. They wanted me to come up with lyrics that would cover the events that had happened as much as possible over the series. There wasn't a lot of pause for thought. I settled down for the first show on 20th February with a pen and notepad.

    I realised that to cover as much detail as possible in the four minutes that I'd been given as a guide time, the song was going to have a lot of words. Maybe that could be the gimmick of the song. I took Gilbert and Sullivan's Modern Major General as inspiration, a stupidly quick and word-full composition that I felt would work on the show. I wrote a couple of introductory verses setting up the song then verse three pretty much covered the first episode. The next week I squeezed every item in the whole show into two verses. For the third episode, I was scheduled to be in hospital for a radical neck dissection to get rid of a tumour in my neck along with all the rest of the lymph nodes. I took a pen and notepad with me.

    I sent as much as I'd written after the first three episodes to the producers, pretty happy with the way it was going. That wasn't going to last. I always knew it was going to be a collaboration as whatever I wrote, they needed to try and film around it, plus work out how Ant and Dec would be involved and the rest of the team too. It was decided that instead of the song being sequential with me writing and learning verses as they were broadcast, verses should focus on different aspects of the show such as the guest announcers, the gameshows, the celebrity participation etc. but that would mean that I couldn't finish writing the song until the day of the final show!! Then perform it on live TV in front of millions. Hmmm...

What followed was a major collaboration between myself, the writers who work on the show, the producers and the incredible musician and arranger Steve Sidwell who I've been a fan of since his work with Robbie Williams on his Royal Albert Hall show. The producers gave me a heads-up of the content of the shows that were yet to be broadcast so I could plan as much as possible.

Stupidly, I assumed that as much of the song as possible would be pre-recorded as it would be a mammoth task to learn it and perform it live. Even with the luxury of autocue, there were a lot of words not to mention key changes. But then after a few production meetings, it was decided that most of it would be live. There is a certain buzz and energy that you can't replicate in a pre-recorded segment and with the lack of an actual live audience, I understood why Ant and Dec wanted to do it that way. It wasn't their concern how many sleepless nights it would cause me.

I've looked back at the first version of the song and it bears very little resemblance to what we're performing tonight and that's perfectly ok. There are definitely fewer words and they are definitely sung slower but it's still an epic production number. Steve did an amazing job with the arrangement and now there are backing vocals, live instruments, dancers, and more key changes than in any other song I've ever performed!

I got the train down from Manchester on Thursday and yesterday, Friday, was spent rehearsing the performance. I recognised familiar faces on the crew from BGT and it was lovely to see Ant and Dec again. I'm not entirely sure what their 'secret' is but they are just lovely chaps and we carried on chatting as if we'd seen each other every week. You forget very quickly that they are two of the most successful television stars in the world, and that may be their appeal. Somehow that comes across through your TV screen, ironically, while they are being TV stars.

The logistics of performing most of the song live were crazy. I'm in one shot at the piano in the studio then as soon as the camera cuts away from me I have to run across the studio, backstage, avoid the dancers and lighting guys, through some double doors, down a corridor and jump behind a second piano, all just ahead of Ant and Dec who are right behind me being filmed on a Steadicam, just in time for the camera to get to me as Mo Farrah is wheeled out in a bath and I sing my next line. Then it's back the same route to the studio piano to be ready for my next bit, out of breath but trying to hide it. Crazy!

As with most TV shows and my extensive experience of them (that would be just the three then) there is a lot of hanging about, sometimes for hours and then a burst of adrenaline before more hanging about. That's certainly the case when you're a guest on a show like Saturday Night Takeaway, compounded by Covid. There's no running between dressing rooms sharing the excitement or congregating in bar areas. More sitting on your dressing room sofa writing your diary for a couple of hours, then being called to the studio because they need to record you waving at the camera before returning to your dressing room for more tea and blog writing. Then at 7 o'clock, my dressing room monitor which had been showing a live feed of the studio floor transforms into a regular TV with the theme of the show and the titles running. It was a slightly discombobulating experience to sit there watching the show unfold on the studio floor directly above me, sipping my cup of tea on my sofa as if I was just relaxing at home on a Saturday evening. Except in about an hour, I'd be escorted the two minutes to that very studio and become a part of the show that I was watching.

My phone was dinging with texts from family and friends as my little pre-recorded wave was broadcast. Some commented that my head looked good and they couldn't see the scars, mostly due to the cameras all being on the other side but I appreciated the support. Then it was time to slip on the sequins, secure the in-ear monitor (yuck) and tuck all the cables out of sight before Frosty arrived to take me upstairs. Frosty has been a part of every TV show that I've been on (the same three) and we've become good pals. The production team had very sweetly delivered a large bouquet to my dressing room which unfortunately was too big for me to manage on the train home with all my luggage so Frosty would be earning some brownie points with some Easter flowers for his Wife. I hope she doesn't read this if he hasn't told her where they came from. Mrs Frosty, your husband is a diamond. The posh scented candle that accompanied the flowers did make it into my case though along with most of the snacks that had been thoughtfully left on my dressing table. I'm sure even the wealthiest guests on TV shows still appreciate the freebies.

It was the last commercial break before my performance as I took my place at the piano and Ant and Dec took their seats next to me. This was the home straight. I only had four minutes to fill in front of the live cameras. The lads had just completed 85 minutes of another successful show and it was an insight to see them 'in the zone' compared to how relaxed we had all been over the last couple of days. For thirty years they've been doing this and their focus and dedication are still evident in everything they do which again may help to explain their longevity. Mo Gilligan, this week's guest announcer introduced the End Of The Show Show 'starring Jon Courtenay' and off we went.

I nearly started off looking at the wrong camera (there are so many) but corrected myself just in time and it all seemed to go well from where I was sitting. There was a short respite in the middle of the song as the pre-recorded section outside the studio was broadcast. We filmed that yesterday in weather that didn't suit my little sequin jacket. Trying to sing through shivery teeth and play the piano with shaking hands is not what I imagined showbiz to be all about. Just a few months earlier I had been sitting about twenty feet away from where I was now, still shivering while we recorded the ITV Panto opening number. Through my in-ear monitor, I could hear Ant and Dec shivering too as I quietly muttered into my mic,

"You couldn't do this bloody show in the summer could you?" Just then Alan the floor manager gave his count into the start of recording and Andi Peters came running down the ramp inside his mini-bubble and bumped into the piano hard enough to move it and knock the mic into my teeth. I barely noticed as I marvelled at the complexion of the man that I remember watching on kid's TV 30 years ago. He hasn't aged at all. Maybe those bubbles are a good idea?

Back to the live broadcast and all too soon it was the last big note, confetti, streamers, one more wave to the camera and it was all over. Ant and Dec spent a couple of minutes chatting to the live screens on the wall and then as it was the last show of the series, there were some short speeches from the director and producer and then Ant and Dec thanked everyone and apologised about the lack of a wrap party which I understand have been quite spectacular in the past. I'll add it to my list of Covid Consequences along with not meeting Royalty after the Royal Variety Performance and missing out on Simon's party after winning BGT. Not that I'm complaining, that's two fewer hangovers in my life. Instead, it was back to my dressing room, packing my bags and then my car back to the hotel for a nice bottle of red and an Instagram Live. Just as we were leaving Television Centre and I was starting to reply to messages on my phone I was startled to see lightning outside the car. I looked up to be greeted by a couple of large gents pointing cameras through the window and shouting my name. It took me a minute to realise I was being 'papped'. Still early days for that experience. I look forward to seeing my confused and startled expression in whatever publication they end up in.

Overall it was a fabulous experience. Emmah was slightly disappointed that I wasn't on screen more but it was never going to be the 'End Of The Jon Courtenay Show'. I love the experience of collaborating with people who are the best at what they do and I'm not precious about anything that I create so long as the final result is a good one. Maybe that's not as dominating or forthright as I need to be in this business but it's who I am and I'm OK with that.

Chapter 19
Awards Shows

My manager Jo was eagerly chasing the BGT producers to try and pin down the exact dates for the National Television Awards knowing that as the winner I would be invited to the swanky do at the O2 where everyone who is anyone in the industry shows up to drink and be merry. Some more than others. I wanted to make sure that it wasn't going to clash with any hospital appointments. I remember getting the call just as I was about to take my CBT exam on my motorbike so I was a little distracted. Jo said that unfortunately, the date was going to clash with a show that I was contracted to do at a Butlin's resort. I argued that it would be in Butlins' interest to let me go as the TV exposure would only help to promote my appearances on their stages and luckily they agreed. Emmah and I were very excited, her a little more perhaps as the soap stars have always been her 'friends' when I've been away, sometimes for weeks at a time so she was looking forward to meeting all of them in person. I said we'd treat ourselves and book a room at Claridge's Hotel where we had stayed many years before when I was performing a show there and a room had been included. We were upgraded that time to the Mayfair Suite which usually costs over £4,000 a night! I was hoping that if I dropped that nugget into the conversation with the hotel receptionist it might happen again. (It didn't). Em also wanted to book a professional to do her hair and makeup knowing that the ceremony was to be televised so we went all out.

It was a couple of weeks later when Jo sent me the invite and a glance showed the addition of the letter 'R' between the 'N' and 'T'. This was the National *Reality* Television Awards, a much more low-key affair with a similarly lower budget, a *much* smaller red carpet and zero television cameras in attendance. Still, it was a night out and our Claridge's reservation was non-refundable so while Jo continued chasing the dates for the *actual* NTAs, I accepted the invite to the N*R*TAs.

As soon as Jo let them know that I'd be going, they asked if I'd be available to present one of the awards and of course I said no problem and thank goodness I did… what an experience.

It was shortly after this that Jo announced that I'd been nominated for Best Performance 2020 by the NRTAs. It was only a few weeks until the event and nominations had been released back in 2020 before the ceremony had been postponed due to Covid. I certainly hadn't been on a list back then. This was starting to sound suspicious. Sure enough, looking back at the original nominations, my fellow comedy performer in the BGT final Nabil Abdulrashid was listed. Not to worry, I'll take it. I love an awards ceremony where you just have to accept the invitation to be nominated.

The event was in the Porchester Hall in London. Emmah and I checked in to Claridge's in the afternoon, her hair and makeup were looking fabulous a few hours later and our Uber *Exec* (I told you we were pulling out all the stops) picked us up. Em had a beautiful new dress with dangerously thin straps, one of which gave up its only job just as the car pulled up at the venue and a breast was released. Luckily the six-foot-long red carpet was actually inside the venue and as there were zero paparazzi outside, I managed to run in and grab a safety pin before we made our official entrance.

The small area of red carpet in front of an NRTA logo-ed backdrop was traversed in seconds and we were sat at our table drinking pretty awful wine in plenty of time to meet the people around us sharing our table. I should mention at this point that I very rarely watch any reality TV unless it's by accident because Em has it on in the bedroom. Love Island, Married At First Sight, Big Brother, baking and sewing shows, dancing on or off ice, housewives, anything in

Chelsea or Essex... I don't have a clue. Consequently, I didn't recognise anyone around us, not that faces were the first things that you saw anyway. There was more cleavage and hot-pants action than in a boxing ring before a round started pre-2019. Both Em and I felt ridiculously overdressed. We even considered losing the safety pin, I'm certain no one would have cared.

I was due to present the first award of the evening so just before it all began I was escorted backstage where I was shown into a holding room which overlooked some apartments in the building next door. The room was also filled with aspiring models who were there to walk around the tables presenting canapés and who were all nominated to win an award, the details of which I've completely forgotten. I said a big group hello and then wandered over to the window which was partially open and offering a slight but welcome breeze into the humid room. A couple of the girls started chatting to me asking why I was there and what did I do, and they all seemed very lovely if a little nervous. Not because of me obviously. Even if meeting the winner of a talent show might make the most experienced and beautiful supermodel tremble with desire, they had no idea who I was anyway. They explained that they were all nominated for an award and this was their first experience of an awards show and they were all feeling a little overwhelmed.

I glanced out of the window as we were chatting to be greeted with the sight of a man sitting in an armchair in the room opposite, with his curtains pulled back, furiously masturbating as he watched something on his television. As I stood there staring he glanced over and for a brief moment our eyes met but to give him his due, he didn't miss a stroke. I also managed to not react too spontaneously and simply glanced back to my audience of a dozen models and told them that if they were feeling nervous and wanted a distraction, they should check out the guy opposite tugging one out. Cue a dozen beauties rushing to the window and I assume a massive climax for the guy who obviously got off by being watched.

Rather than enjoy the moment with my new beautiful friends I was promptly escorted out of the room and stood in the wings next to a table holding all the awards for the evening. The one that I was to present was put in my hand as I waited to hear my name introduced. I was waiting long enough to glance down at the table and see the closest one had my name on it. 'Performance of the Year 2020, Jon Courtenay'. With the surprise of my win well and truly spoilt, I walked on stage and looked out over a sea of botox, boobs and butt fillers and ad-libbed something along the lines of:

"There is a great body of work represented here tonight and some great work on bodies too."

Nothing. I blamed the shoddy PA system and got on with the presenting. Afterwards I was escorted back to my table where I broke the news to Emmah that we couldn't sneak out before the end because I'd won the award that I was only recently nominated for. So we got pissed on the awful wine instead. Bizarrely no one really spoke to us for the entire evening. Even when I returned to our table of a dozen people clutching my newly won trophy, not a single glance or word from any of our table mates. We'd made an effort too, it's not like either myself or Em are shy chatting to people but after a while I think we realised that even less people knew me than I knew any of them so we spent the evening slyly getting photos of all the flesh on display instead. I did mange to say a quick hello to Claire Sweeny and Brendan Cole before they sneaked out and left early and thankfully we had the luxury of Claridge's to return to while we pretended to still be posh at the end of the evening.

I don't want to sound ungrateful. It's still clear on my website that I was the recipient of The National Reality Television Award

Performance of the Year 2020 in the hope that some people will misread it like Jo did originally.

But then finally along came the actual NTAs. Having blown our hotel budget the month before, we were going to book something a lot more down to earth before my mate Dean Andrews pointed out that if I'd been invited to the ceremony then a hotel and car should be included. Dean and I had met years before when he was performing on a cruise ship but he already had a lot of acting roles under his belt and it wasn't long before he landed a big part in Emmerdale. Having not ever watched the show, it was a funny moment when Em paused the TV one evening to go and pour a glass of something and it froze on Dean's face and I nonchalantly commented:

"Ha. That's not a good shot of Dean."

"Who?" She replies,

"That bloke," I explain, pointing at the screen.

"He's called Will."

"He may be called Will on the show but his real name is Dean. He's a mate."

"You know Will Taylor?"

"No, I know Dean Andrews."

This went on for a while with Emmah asking me why I hadn't mentioned it before etc… but it was good to know that I'd have at least one proper mate at the ceremony. More hair and makeup was booked for the afternoon and our car dropped Emmah and myself along with my manager Jo at one end of the red carpet a couple of hours before the show was due to start.

Now this was a proper red carpet, about 100m long with press and cameras down one side and the public with camera phones at the ready on the other. We opened the car door and stepped onto the carpet and I was perfectly prepared to just walk down it and get in to the venue. No one had told us any differently but apparently there is an art to this kind of thing and we needed some training. A kind lady with a clipboard must have spotted our slightly bemused expressions and pointed out that we should zigzag our way down chatting to press on one side and taking selfies with the public on the other. She walked me to a camera and presenter on one side but failed to introduce me to the guy holding the mic who fumbled his way through a few questions without hiding the fact that he'd never watched BGT before. It was awkward. So I zagged to the other side where a couple of people were calling my name and took a few selfies and then zigged back to the press side and spoke to another person who barely hid the fact that she'd rather be chatting to Ruth Langford or Ross Kemp who were a little ahead of us. Ruth was actually very lovely and came to Em's rescue when she noticed her doing that thing people do when their eyes start to water and they've paid £200 for professional makeup. A cotton swab magically appeared as Ruth announced:

"I come prepared for everything on a red carpet."

Oiled by the bottle of bubbly at the hotel, Em stood chatting to Ruth like a couple of girlfriends waiting at a bus stop while I continued with selfies and chat. Then she got a little more excited when she glanced behind her and shouted "Hi" whilst waving at a guy a good twenty feet away and off she trotted to give him a big hug. Jo turned to me:

"I think Em knows someone on the red carpet."

I didn't recognise the guy that she was chatting animatedly to but didn't have time to dwell on it as I continued negotiating the zigging and zagging including randomly patting Stephen Mulhern on the arse as he chatted to the BBC. (We'd shared makeup chairs before the Royal Variety so somehow I thought an arse slap would be appropriate.) After a while Em rejoined me and I had the chance to ask who her friend was.

"I don't know his real name but he's on Casualty and he's really good."

In the absence of an emoji, just imagine me face-palming myself.

"You just accosted a guy on the red carpet while you were also on the red carpet because you're a fan?" I asked incredulously. "He must have thought some crazed member of the public had jumped the barriers!"

That's really all you need to know about my Wife. In the words of Forest Gump, that's all I really have to say about that.

The rest of the night was good fun although the endless supply of free booze does knock down the inhibitions of even a slightly socially awkward, natural introvert like me. Asking Holly Willoughby if I could smell her and then waiting what seemed like a lifetime before she recognised me as the guy that wrote the slightly stalker-ish song about her the year before, wasn't a highlight. Then realising we were sat just two rows behind Ricky Gervais and thinking it would be a good opportunity to tell him about the time he cost me £2,000 is also something I probably shouldn't boast about in a book. [10]

---

[10] It's not a particularly riveting story to anyone, let alone Ricky. About 15 years earlier, Em had made it to the finals of giftwrapper-of-the-year on Good Morning with Richard and Judy and with no bias whatsoever I can tell you that Em should have walked away with the £2,000 Christmas gift voucher. Judy however didn't like the fact that Richard voted for the prettiest one (my Mrs) so she chose one of the others and it was down to that morning's guest on the sofa to decide. Ricky did the only diplomatic thing and chose the third finalist. For some reason, telling Ricky that story at the front of the O2 in the middle of the National Television Awards took about ten minutes. Despite him being nothing but polite and gracious, I slunk back to my seat and put my head in my hands, mortified.

Chapter 20
Belt And Braces

My consultant recommended that I swap back to NHS treatment for my immunotherapy given that each session costs tens of thousands of pounds privately. I agreed that would be a good idea and I was put under the care of one of the leading Professors dealing with the treatment. It was explained that my type of cancer had a 50/50 chance of returning but with a year's course of immunotherapy, those odds were reduced to 80-90% in favour of living longer. So again, despite them having to read me the list of potential side effects, it was, in the common vernacular, a no-brainer.

Potential side effects of immuno; I shall abbreviate it from now on as my eyes go funny when I have to type it; do not include your eyes going funny. Unlike chemotherapy and radiotherapy, immuno can affect any organ as there is no chemical or radiological therapy aimed directly at cancer cells. Instead, it encourages your own immune system to fight the little bastard cancer cells. My body scans could only recognise unwelcome lumps, growths, tumours etc, over 5mm in diameter. The thinking was that immuno would take care of anything that the scans couldn't see. The list of common side effects is arthritis, chills, constipation, coughing, decreased appetite, diarrhoea, fatigue, fever and flu-like symptoms, headache, itching, muscle aches, nausea, rashes and vomiting. (Thank you Cancer Research UK website). I was very lucky and suffered some minor skin rashes/itching and a little fatigue. More severe side effects include symptoms with longer words: colitis, hepatitis, inflammation of the lung, (pneumonitis), kidney failure, myocarditis or inflammation of the heart, neuropathy, paralysis, meningitis, or encephalitis, pancreatitis, severe infections, severe skin reactions and type 1 diabetes.

So far I've suffered nothing that I can't spell.

I have to say at this point that the treatment I was given on the NHS was absolutely exemplary. If I was in America, this course of treatment, scans and checkups would no doubt have bankrupted me despite winning a chunk of cash on a TV show. Every nurse, doctor, consultant and janitor at Christie's Hospital was a delight to interact with and every day I was there I marvelled at these people who had trained for years in order to help keep the rest of us alive longer, most of them for a lot less money than they deserve.

Before I started writing this book, I wrote a new show. It's the story that you've read here but it only lasts forty-five minutes and it all rhymes. I was told it might be a good fit for the Edinburgh Fringe Festival, an event that I've only attended once and then as a punter, not a performer. I was asked many times after winning BGT what I was hoping to do in the future and my answer was always the same; I wanted to get back into acting. I was involved with a youth theatre when I was sixteen and absolutely loved it and had every intention of attending drama school but then started getting paid to do something else that I loved when I was visiting my parents in Cyprus and everything just escalated from there. Maybe Edinburgh will open some acting doors that BGT didn't and maybe I get to show off my acting chops. Although I'm not sure how much acting is involved when the story is true and it happened to you. Isn't that just more re-living than acting?

My reasons for writing the show were the same as for writing this book. From a selfish perspective, it's great therapy to get my thoughts on paper whether it's a book or a script and I've realised a lot since writing began. From a wider perspective, I think it's a good thing to talk about it all and to keep it honest. One in two of us will suffer from cancer in our lives and most of us will be affected by it indirectly. I know that talking about it was one of the best medicines I had during my treatment. Not all of us are lucky enough to have loved ones around us when we go through the toughest of times, hopefully we have a friend or two but even then there are things you may only discover when you talk to a stranger so a big thank you to all the therapists, psychologists and psychiatrists out there who help those in need.

I know it's a cliché that men don't talk about their feelings but I may have mentioned my thoughts about clichés earlier on, they're often true. I don't want to limit it to men either, especially in this day and age of gender neutral personages. At the risk of alienating every other country, let's just open it up to the British in general. We're not great at showing our feelings or talking about them so as awkward as my heart-on-my-sleeve book and subsequent show may make a few people feel, if it makes anyone who is going through something similar realise that they're not alone then that's worth a little buttock-squirming isn't it?

Thanks for reading part of my story. If you'd like to get in touch with me directly with anything other than mean words, you can email againsttheoddsbook@gmail.com

Macmillan's number is 0808 239 1557.

When you can be anything in this life, be kind.

Appendix
Against The Odds
The One-Man Musical

The stage is a simple set with a white chair centre stage, a white coat stand with jackets on stage left and a white grand piano with stool. There is a 'mirror' frame on a tall stand stage right. There are lights around the mirror frame facing the audience which are lit, there are also lights on the other side. When the lights are switched over, a person can 'appear' in the mirror.

[Jon appears in the mirror shaving. He sings to himself:]
The Mole Song

Every mole could be, potentially
An invitation to the Big C
So get them checked periodically
It could make a difference take it from me

Maybe it's big when it's used to be small
Maybe it's colour has changed from before
Maybe there's not any difference at all
But while you're there check your boobs or your balls

Don't let your concerns sit unresolved,
Our self awareness has evolved
Catch it early it's probably solved,
Make it fun get your partner involved

Jump in the shower and play hunt the mole,
Check every cranny and nook and hole
Showering for two is the new rock and roll,
See what comes up if you lose control

They'll cut out a mole with a small anaesthetic,
There's not any pain so don't be pathetic
You only live once, don't let cancer wreck it.
If you've got a lump or a mole: go and check it

[He then nicks the side of his head which hurts him, he drops the razor to the floor. Razor is on a thread attached to mirror for end of show]

[Beat]
My face and head
Smooth before bed
But foam's mixed with red
Blood, from a nick
What a dick
You'd think I know
The direction it grows
No such luck
This schmuck
Gets distracted
And in fact he
Now stops.
Because this nick, not old,
Is from a new mole
Near my earhole.

I should have called my doctor
But I forgot or
Life got in the way
Suffice to say
I just decide
To quietly slide
Between the sheets and hide.
My intention not to mention
The mole for fear of ridicule.
Besides, the next day is gonna be cool.

[Jon stands to the side of the stage, puts on his blue jacket and speaks first line to the wings as he walks to centre stage]

Hello Ant & Dec, you singular icon
How does this work? Do I just walk on?

Hello Simon, my name's Jon
I'm a pianist, and I'm from
A small village near Avon.
[aside]
Not really but it rhymed. Could have been Azerbaijan.
This, judges, is my audition song.

3RD PERSON

There was a man who had a dream,
That Simon Cowell and his team
Would see him play the piano and try to slay them,
On the stage of the Palladium
And in the time that one song took,
David would write another children's book.
Alesha would smile at him, Amanda would be kind to him,
Simon's teeth would be blinding him
But nothing now could ever spoil,
The dream he dreamed, like Susan Boyle.

The fact is he never thought he'd ever get to be;
In front of millions of people doing his thing on TV
30 years of playing in piano bars and pubs;
Dodging glasses when they're thrown, being thrown out of clubs.
When he realises he's older and fifty ain't so far;
And he's having trouble making all the payments on his car.
And his children ask "Daddy, when are you coming home?"
This game is not the same when you're just 'Daddy on the phone'.

So he sits at the piano and he tries to get prepared;
Thinking he'll write it in 3rd person so he doesn't feel as scared
To sing about himself to a bunch of strangers in the dark
But then Britain has got talent and these people left their mark:

Paul Potts won the first year and said it was insane
The second year George Sampson won, singing in the rain.
Diversity won the 3rd year, then the world would see

A dancing dog, he stole our hearts, when the winner was Pudsey
Lost Voice Guy season 12, and last year Colin Thackery…
So why not me?

That's what he said; His youngest boy one night in bed.
"Dad… why not you? Go and show them what you do…
And even though you'll be a wreck; At least you'll meet Ant and Dec."
And that's when he tells his son, he has to admit
When he meets Ant and Dec how does he know which is which
If Ant is the tall one then Dec must be
The other one. Obviously.

And then he thinks on stage; at this stage in his life
With an expensive mortgage and a pensive wife,
His youngest son, Alfie says "What's it all about?"
If he had any hair left he'd pull it out…
His teenage son said: "Ugh, ugh, ughhh"

His Dad taught him to play piano but he didn't live to see
His son in the famous theatre performing on TV.
If he didn't see it through, imagine how sad,
The look on the faces of both his lads
Who always tells him "you're the greatest showman Dad"

And they'll see me, on BGT
No more third person, just 'Daddy':
This is me.

[Beat]
The Palladium audience are on their feet,
The judges say things so sweet
Ant and Dec hit the buzzer and greet
Me on stage.

Then there's too much excitement, too much to do
This mid-life career success long overdue,
When it's broadcast months later, people view
Me, on their TV screens,

And it all seems
That my dreams have come true.
And all thoughts of that mole, misshapen and new
Are forgotten. So the rotten cells break through.

Plus by now every persona
From London to …Barcelona
From Alaska to Arizona
Through those TV screens are shown a
Spiky red blob called Corona
So my mole thinks: "I'm gonna grow on ya"

[Jon puts on a baseball cap to play the part of 'Troll', and opens a laptop on top of the piano. He swigs from a can of beer and tosses it away.]

I may be faceless as I criticise
That variety of vomit that was televised.
Sentimental shit thrust before my eyes
I only wanna see Amanda's cleavage size.

If you're so clever then take the words
Written in the social media 'verse
Aided by Musk and Zuckerburg
And write a song that we haven't heard.

[Jon removes the baseball cap]

Ok then my angry, faceless twin…
Imagine how mad he'll be when I go on to win?

All these comments are real though hopefully not true
Although they're shitty, I don't want pity, I got lots of nice ones too.

BALDY WITH A BUZZER

I wrote a little song that was on TV
For my audition on BGT
Thanks to Dec and Anthony
Things for me got a little crazy.
I wasn't quite set for the media frenzy
On Insta, Facebook, YouTube and Twittery
So many people supportive and loverly,
Thanks to you it means a lot to me.
But for every Skywalker, there's Darth Vader,
You can't avoid the keyboard crusader
Gotta take the bad with the good they tell you,
Got this type of material from a few:

[as troll with cap on typing on phone]
'He's a bit un-amusing', 'he just can't sing', 'I fink he is irritating'
'He didn't deserve it', 'he's annoying', 'I am really not enjoying.'
'His songwriting is bad and sloppery', 'He can't play piano properly'
'I could do what he is doing if I could play piano or sing'. Obviously.

'What a load of rubbish' that's invaluable.
'Never heard of him before' that's understandable
'Shouldn't have got the buzzer' it was quite incredible.
'He won't make the finals' that's short-fightable.
'I'm stickin 2 it' number 2 that's numerable.
'A baldy with a buzzer' that's quite memorable!

[Cap off]
Baldy with a buzzer, yes sir that's me,
Baldy with a buzzer, through to the semi
Baldy with a buzzer, incredibly.
Baldy with a buzzer and his family.... thank you.

Some people feel that they have to share
Every opinion everywhere
And often feel the need to swear
Sat in underwear in an old armchair.

I was told as a child if you can't say something
Kind then maybe you shouldn't say anything
Mind your words, your Ps and Q-ing,
No vitriol spewing while You Tube viewing.
It's not nice to hurt it doesn't hurt to be nice.
Before words spurt forth maybe think twice,
Trolls once hid in Norwegian Fjords,
Now they hid behind their keyboards:

[cap on and typing on phone]
'Nah he made the judges guilty',
'Looks like the guy from the pawn shop to me.'
'Why did he get the golden buzzer seriously?',
'Looks like grown up Bob from Nativity'
'He's too old to be on TV',
'I hate him more than anchovy'
'He's like Marmite if you don't like Marmite',
'I'll keep it short and concise: Utter shite.'

[cap off]
'So unfunny' that's not comical.
'I wouldn't pay to see him' that's economical
'He'll never be a star' that's astronomical.
'I hope he disappears' that would be magical.
'I'd like to slap him' let's get physical.
'A baldy with a buzzer', that's still topical:

Baldy with a buzzer, I'm that chappie,
Baldy with a buzzer, I'm quite happy
Baldy with a buzzer, paparazzi
Make sure you spell it correctly
Baldy with a buzzer…. thank you.

[Jon on phone]
Hi, is this the producer of BGT?
Yeah I know I called you, you didn't call me
But I need to establish who you are you see,
In case anyone is listening, obviously.

[glancing at the audience and making a 'shh' gesture]

So I wrote a great song back in January
[Covers mouthpiece and speaks to audience:]
It's now early March, 2020
[Back to phone]
It's called 'I Must Not Die' it's funny
It's all about how I could potentially
Ruin this momentous televisual opportunity.
Like I could break my arm or get poorly,
Or I could die, that would surely be
A problem for my job security.
[Covers mouthpiece and speaks to audience:]
I also wrote it ironically
Before covid was even heard of and before cancer found me.
'I Must Not Die', I know right? Crazy.
[To phone]
Yes, of course you need to hear it,
I'll play it immediately.

I MUST NOT DIE

On the edge of my success, I don't want to make a mess
Of this opportunity that I have got.
In these crazy circumstances, I don't want to take chances
With my Britain's Got Talent Semi-Final spot
I can't think of any reason, why for this 14th season
I couldn't be a possible hotshot
The only problem I can see, could ruin any chance for me
Is if I'm dead, and I've thought of this a lot.
I must not die. That would be quite traumatic
If I die, it would be problematic
So I'll try, to remain emphatically alive…
I must not die.

My career could bounce back from an assortment of setbacks
I could maybe stub my finger or my toe
I could get a broken nail or there are many kind of ail-

-Ments which would never make a difference to my show.
I'm hoping that the Pearly Gates will want to make my visit late
Although Heaven's Got Talent undoubtedly
But I want to live to be the big branch on my family tree
So my grandchildren can see my spot on B. G. T…

I must not die. That would be the final curtain
If I die, then I think I'm fairly certain
That I'd cry, though my eyes would not be workin' they'd be dry.
I must not die.

Since I was on TV, I've had advice from family
With the greatest of intentions I am sure
Don't experiment with chemicals, socialise with cannibals,
Or catch a disease without a cure
It's not on my agenda to put hands inside a blender
Or drink water that is any way impure.
So it must be safe to say that at the end of every day
I stand a good chance that my life will still endure…

And now the bridge, I'm gonna croon, this is the bit of song that's got a different tune,
But bridges can be, another fatality,
Like a bridge over troubled water,
London Bridge is falling down,
The rope bridge groans in Indiana Jones, but Indy didn't die…

Just like James Bond, you always can rely
The bullets always miss him when they fly
Leaving him to wittily reply:
"No Miss Moneypenny, I don't expect to die.

"Old school, Sean Connery, I can't do Daniel Craig. My Wife wants to!"
Dead like Shakespeare's Romeo, Muffassa killed by buffalo,
Don't want to be a cameo, or underneath a patio
Just wanna play the piano and make it to another show.
That's why… I did not die!

[A foam prop-light mounted above Jon falls and knocks him to the floor. Lying on the floor still, Jon shouts at the phone on the piano:]

Hello? Hello? Are you still there?
No of course I'm very aware
That you may think, or it may seem
I wrote that in poor taste but I mean
I wrote it months before lockdown started
When the thought of anyone dying was more light hearted.
Yes of course there's a pandemic, and I know
That I can't do it in the show
I'll do it another time that's for sure
Like when I'm on tour in 2024.

[Jon puts on a doctors scrub cap to play the part of 'Surgeon' who is French]

Hello Jon,
I am your sur-geon,
I did the opera-tion
And your mole is gone.
Biopsy says cancer
But for me I fancy ya
Chances. With a skin graft
But we are understaffed
So there is a delay
And we cannot say
If the cancer has found a way
To places not found today.
I will send a letter
When I know better
What I can do.
Toodle-oo.

[Jon removes scrub cap]
So I need to write a new song
To replace the one that's gone
In the bin:

'I must not die'.
Now more of a maxim.

[Beat]
I'm not sure who is to blame
For what happened in the studio when my time came
To record the semi-finals. It was a shame
'Cos I'd rehearsed for months, they called my name
And the virtual wall Clapped and cheered
My nerves as bad as I'd feared
Then I was on and it appeared
To be going well.
But then at the first hurdle, I fell…

The photo of me
On the giant LED
And I quipped on the night
I'm the one on the right
Although I did see a sight
Of a woman who might
Have been left bereft
After plastic surgery:
She looked like the one on the left.

WHEN I WAS A BOY PART 1

One day I dreamed I might be on TV
That people would wave when they recognised me
Then I made it on screen but it must be a hoax
I'm just a piano man with a bunch of bad Dad jokes. *[Longest hair]*

People ask me why I do this, then they understood
Inspiration from Chaplin to Victoria Wood
As a child I saw variety shows on the screen
Wanting to be Billy Connelly, Elton or Queen.

My hair no longer grows,
Just out my ears and out my nose,
My body makes noises I'm such a wreck
My forehead now has met my neck

Some things go together like Robin and Batman
Like Mac and cheese, like Simon and fake tan.
But the greatest double act the world ever had:
Was Carolyn and Ivan, that's my Mum and Dad.

They were on stage long before I was born
As a child I would sit there just shouting for more
They'd take me backstage and naked dancers I'd see
I decided show business was the business for me

[There is a long pause]

That was the moment, it happened so fast,
Barely even noticeable in the broadcast.
But in my mind a total CALAMITY!
The enormity of this opportunity
Came crashing down on top of me.
Or perhaps the reason could possibly be
That Amanda was smiling quite happily
But due to a lighting technicality
I realised her dress was totally
Utterly and completely translucent. Tastefully.

[Jon puts the baseball cap on for one line as Troll]
Aw I wish I could see.

[Jon removes baseball cap]
Shut up troll. You disgust me.

So though well impressed
With the outline of breast
None the less
It had made me digress.

What content
Was I meant
To sing next?
Like the moment of climax for any man here.
I couldn't think straight my brain slipped a gear.
And unlike Amanda's lovely brassier,
I was empty. *[beat]*

Maybe the causality
Was due to my infirmity
And the dread of my mortality
But what a time to come to me,
But lets go back in time,
And you'll see what I'm
Going to attempt to play
Is what I should have done that day
And you can hear it the way
That I wrote the damn thing. Ok…

[Back to piano]

WHEN I WAS A BOY PART 2

I'll keep all the photos as I'm growing old
Because memories like this are more precious than gold.
I made an album so that I can reminisce when I look
Then I go back to putting pictures of my dinner on Facebook.

When I was eleven, in my first spot light
I was nervous and shaking and damning stage fright
But I knew this was it, this was my life, for me,
So I let out a breath… and a little bit of wee.

He'd taught me piano, I'd watched them both sing
I'd seen the laughter they gave and the applause that it brings.
And though they dreamed of fame and to be on TV
They were always the biggest stars in the world to me.

For forty-five years they were barely apart
But there wasn't a day when I didn't hear them laugh
Like when Dad dropped a glass of chocolate milk in the bath
When we saw the mess he said "I only meant to fart!"

Dad was still laughing until his final bow
And the memories of him make us laugh even now
Mum said "Never give up" and she knows I love her,
But even she never dreamed I'd get the golden buzzer!!!

My children have watched me from their youngest age,
Bringing music and laughter from up on the stage,
Just like I watched my Mum, so her dream comes true now
She gets to be on TV, virtually. Mum, take a bow…

Your family may be crazy, they may drive you round the bend
And your kids may drive you insane, it's a never ending spend,
But my Mum always taught me, "Be proud of who you are"
So now I teach my children, always reach for the star.

[Jon stays at piano]

When those lyrics decided to depart
That led to my head having that brain fart
That tensed my arse and stopped my heart
Covered by the producer's skill and art
And my slip was broadcast as barely a blip.
But at the time, I was ready to quit.

"And now I tell my children, always reach for the star..ah…ah…ahhh…"

[Centre stage:]

My head pounded,
I jumped up and bounded
From the studio floor,
Rounded the corner and saw:

'Exit'. That would do.
Past surprised television crew,
Past a security guard I flew
Until fresh air where my hair once grew
Hit me and then I knew
I could let my pent up tears come through.
I sobbed like a dog without a toy to chew
Convinced I'd screwed it.
Somehow knew it.
My big chance and I blew it.
Fuck!
Cried like a baby without a breast,
Like a chick without a nest,
Like I was at an onion-chopping contest.

But, I would never have guessed
That this song,
That went so wrong,
Luckily was original
My own composition will
Be my saving grace.
And I save face
When no judge in the place
Knows that I messed up.
And they choose me
In the top three
And then the act to be
Sent directly
To the finals show.
What do ya know?
All this with a hole where my mole used to be,
This is me.

[Jon removes jacket and puts the scrub cap back on as Surgeon
Your appointment is overdue
This is the third attempt because you
Have managed since June
With misfortune

To contract Covid, twice and sad but true
Sometimes the malignancy burns through
Long after it's gone. So the tests argue
That the cancer has not bid adieu.

[Jon removes scrub cap and sits in chair. He begins driving]

FAR QUEUE CANCER

Another visit to the hospital,
The sat nav now isn't used at all
I've travelled this route a few times before,
Another visit to the hospital

Directed to yet another door,
Another queue on another floor
Another doctor who knows it all,
Another visit to the hospital

But this time there are so many people.
Some eyes show pain but some will keep all
Their suffering inside and quiet.
Won't flaunt their gauntness from the cancer diet.

Now I've lost my sense of direction,
A nurse catches my unsure expression
So many lines in front of so many doors,
Sickness has never been this popular before.

"Is it cancer?" She asks, and then she's at it:
"Is it throat or neck? Or pancreatic?
This line for drugs that treat infertility,
This queue for pains and immobility,
This line for dementia and general senility."
Like a traffic cop, she points ridiculously,
"Stop!" I shout and make her look at me.
You had me at cancer, which queue is it for me?
"The furthest one" as she points finally.

"The far queue?" I ask as if it's meant to be.

Far queue cancer, far queue. Far queue cancer, far queue.
I'll join the line that I'm assigned for malignant tumours not benign.
I feel resigned that it's a sign.

Far queue cancer, far queue. Far queue cancer, far queue.
Fuck you. Fuck you. FUCK YOU!

[spoken]
Hello Doctor….

An aside here despite my consternation
To portray in rhyming explanation
The characteristics of my surgeon. My fascination
With this brilliant man is a combination
Of wonder at his dedication
To rid patients of cancerous abominations
Combined with his solid, unwavering conviction,
That Covid and it's treatment is a work of fiction.

Unwavering and often as not unmasked
Never once did I hear him ask
Could you pass the sanitising gel?
Seriously! What the Hell?
What is he thinking, other than
"If you've got cancer, I'm your man,
But Corona is just a scam.
It will stop quicker than it began."

Also, unfortunately for me
Hoping as I was, that some priority
Would be given to this new 'celebrity'
He doesn't own a TV.

His nurse is called Emma, same name as my Wife
She senses the darkness consuming my life
And unlike my doctor with no TV

She's a huge fan of BGT
And whispers in my ear discreetly:

[Jon puts on a nurses hat to play the part of 'Nurse']
Could you sign something for me?

This must be the highlight of your career
But your health is as low as you could possibly fear.
It seems to me that psychologically, this year
You must be a mess. And I shed a tear.

[Jon removes the nurses hat and sits in the chair]
Then, unlike my doctor, so quick to shake hands,
She glances behind, takes her chance and stands
And hugs me. Ignoring reprimands.
And I sob as I realise that I understand
Why I feel lost. And alone. And in quicksand.

[Jon puts red jacket on]
So now I have two appointment dates,
First the finals show in October then straight
To hospital where a scalpel awaits
My career and my health: Two unknown fates.

I don't know how much I need to say
But career-wise, my fate went OK.
The song I wrote seemed to hit the note
And 35 percent of the viewers gave me the winning vote.

SMALL THINGS

Moments in your life don't get much bigger than this,
It's a milestone, like a wedding, or a teenager's first kiss.
But to be here in the finals is feeling slightly odd
It's champagne and caviar I'm used to Vimto and battered cod.

And while this moment overwhelms me, the question must be asked
Do we sometimes miss the small things as life goes by so fast

Mosquitos are only tiny but they can drive you mad
So never underestimate small things that make you glad
My Wife makes me happy and she'll be there if I call
I got undressed and she got stressed when she realised it's just small

Things like the last shoes in the sale are the right size for you.
A baby's expression when they're having a poo,
Looking in a junk drawer and finding a pen
Fitting a size 8 when you are usually a 10.

Small things that make you happy, small things that make you laugh,
Bubbles make kids giggle when they're trumping in the bath.
Aardvarks are happy when it's alphabetical,
Dogs will always wag their tails if they can lick their

Ballgames make kids happy when they're playing having fun
I wasn't happy when the schools closed and I had to teach my sons.
I was happy when Boris told me I could finally hug my Mum
But I was happiest in lockdown finding loo roll for my bum.

Ant and Dec are happy when they take home an award
So they've been pretty happy since 1994.
You want to seize the moment, 'You just live once' I hear you say
But that's not true… you die once, but you must live every day.
Smile as if they've told you there's no need to quarantine
When you laugh in denim… happiness is in your genes.

Happiness is small things like being with our friends
Little things like when the Queen said we'll meet again
On Thursdays, on doorsteps with pride inside our chests
Taking just a moment to clap the NHS.

And it won't be long before the masks are gone,
We'll be living life to the maximum
And we'll remember people like Sir Captain Tom,
And in years our kids will be reminiscing,
Not about big stuff that they've been missing
But that every day they got to play with Dad and Mum.

And we'll remember that we were strong
When McDonalds was closed for so very long
And Britain's talent will be that we all carry on.
And Britain's talent will be that we all carry on.

To be here now, to get this far, for you to make me feel like a star,
For gratitude I don't know where to start
When Alfie asked me "What's it all about"
I thought I knew but I had my doubts,
But the answer is so simple and so smart:
You'll realise through it all, the moments that you thought were small,
Can take the biggest places in your heart.
And if you're lucky your family plays the biggest part.

[Red jacket off]
Then straight to scalpel
And so there's no gamble
They remove ample
Scalp and the sample
Tissue's sent away,
And there's more delay
But they say OK
Wait to hear what they say

LONG TIME COMING

Since Dad first taught me how to play and I wrote my first song
From the jokes that I began to write and the nights they went so wrong
From an audience of five or six, to driving home alone
Finding a love that understood, having children of my own.

Just a bit of fun when my youngest son said "Give yourself a chance"
Never thought I'd be on BGT, I'm not a dog and I can't dance
Then the Palladium, an ovation, in front of my kids and Wife
And now at night, alone with fright, I don't want to leave this life.

It's been a long time coming but now my chance is here

It's the world that I've been hoping for, it's finally appeared
But now my fear
Has fuck all to do with my career
How do I tell my kids
They could only have me for another year?

I MUST NOT DIE REPRISE.

I must not die
That would be quite traumatic if I die
It could be problematic so I'll try
To remain emphatically alive.
I must not die.

[Beat. Jon as 'Producer' appears on screen]
The new preferred method of communication
Due to pandemic ramifications
And the wish that with hind-sightification
We'd all bought shares in the Zoom application.

[Producer]
Hello Jon, I'm producing
The show that this year will be using
You because you won Sir,
So speaking as the producer
I need to sweet talk and seduce ya
Because this won't be the show that you're been used to

[Jon]
Oh I'm not used to anything you see
I've only ever watched it on TV
Albeit every year since I was three
Maybe younger, it's a huge deal for me.
Come on, it's the Royal Variety
I get to talk with Royalty

[Producer]
Ah well that's the thing, Jon

Some of that may be gone, Jon
Covid goes on and on
But so does the show Jon
We don't want to abandon
Over 100 years of traditi-on
I love your background… what's it on?

[Jon, looking behind him at the audience]

It's *[local town]* audience,
Part of the new Zoom experience
It replaced Golden Gate Bridge on the upgrade since
No one really used it. Wince.

[Producer leans forward and changes his Golden Gate background to 'messy office']

[Producer]
Great, well as I was said,
We really can't risk the spread
Of Corona to the head
Of the Country. We'll have Charles, instead.

[Jon]
So it's fine for the next in line?

[Producer]
He won't actually be there, for real
It'll be a recording, we'll
Project it. On screen. Because we feel
It's safer. Although with less appeal.

[Jon]
Well for the audience that is there it's still a big deal.

[Producer]
Yes, about the audience, we need to chat
There may be another problem with that

It's not exact-ly the format that we
Would like ideally,
But there'll be no audience. Theatrically.

[Jon]
I don't understand. The theatre's empty?

[Producer]
Nooo… no no no, not exactly.
TV screens where the audience would be
So you'll still be able to see
Faces. Like now. You can see me.

[Jon]
Seriously? The Royal Variety…
With no royals, a Zoom call basically?

[Producer]
Yeah. But with Mich n Steps don't we?

[Jon]
I've been in one of them, actually.
Crass but true, back in the day
Long before Steps, I used to date Faye.
I know right? Look at me! No way!

[Jon at piano]
December 2020, feigning Christmas cheer
Months of diazepam, whiskey and fear,
Behind fake brave eyes, holding kids near,
The hospital phones: It's all clear.

FAR QUEUE CANCER REPRISE   *[Jon at piano]*

Far queue for cancer, far queue.
far queue cancer, far queue.
Fuck you. Fuck you. FUCK YOU!

[Beat]
The next four weeks at least are a charm
Then as I sit at my piano, my neck on my arm,
A small alarm as I feel subtlely
A lump where no lump used to be.
Oh fuck me. Another biopsy
An eternity, the wait to see
What I anticipate accurately
Is cunting cancer's return in me.

More nights to dry my eyes
Macallan drunk, McMillan therapise
Therapists more wise than I
recognise my pain and analyse
My brain. So I will summarise
With this refrain:

TUMOUR TWO SONG

I need a a radical dissection on the side of my neck
59 stitches and a scar, I'm a wreck
Doctors are perplexed they all say what the heck?
We were certain that it hadn't spread.

A theatre again but no pi-an-o
Again in a spotlight but this time I know
My audience is an anaesthetist as I go
To sleep on this operation bed

For 8 hours, did I dream of the possibilities
They'd told me potentially I'd suffer if one of these
Surgeons cut the wrong nerve despite their expertise
"We could paralyse your face," they'd said.

Eight hours that passed in the blink of an eye
Which luckily still blinked when they opened and I
Turned to Emma the nurse and croaked eloquently "Hi,"
I guess I'm ok and not dead?"

I guess, I'm ok, and not dead? I guess I'm ok, and not dead.

BREATHLESS

[Beat]
One month later as I recover
One afternoon I discover
A slight, inconvenient bother:
I can't get a breath.

Having experienced anxiety
So prevalent in society
I assume this is a variety
Of that. Or it's death.

An ambulance is quickly dispatched
From Emmah (the Wife, not nurse) I'm snatched
Oxygen is firmly attached
To A&E

Where I'm dealt with by another nurse
Who is by no means averse
To making an effort to converse.
She's a fan apparently.

The problem you can imagine
This situation that I'm in
Where I can't breathe to chime in:
"I love that you're a fan.

But could you hold the conversation
Until you've found the causation
Of my breathless situation
Then I'm your man".

"I'm so sorry," she continues
"I watched all your interviews
"I even voted for you-s,

Do you speak to Simon anymore?"

A thumbs up is all I can muster
By now dizzy and lacklustre
I see stars in a distant cluster
As I pass out on the floor.

My lung collapsed due to infection
Re-inflated with air injection
Colour returns to my complexion
NHS sublime.

A year of immunotherapy
Gave me time to write what you've heard from me
Everyone here has their story
Thank you for being part of mine.

NOT THE FINAL SONG

It's a life so far that's splendid
Though at times I may have tended
To wear rose coloured spectacles
To treat problems as hypotheticals.
But against the odds I'm here. With scars but all clear.

It's a show that hasn't ended
That one day may be appended
In real life a happy ending
Is really just depending
On how you persevere. On how love holds you near.

Your story can't be over if you're telling it
However hard the graft, heart-breaking or compelling it
Goes on. It goes on.

We all want a happy ending but our ends are all impending
So find happiness along the way and on that final judgement day

When you go on. If you go on,
You can say the life you've spent,
Is one lived without repent.
I hope you loved and were loved in return.

And I hope this testimonial
Will live on beyond millennials
I hope whoever gets to write
The final chapter of my life
Gets it right.
This chapter ends tonight.
How it *should* have started.
Good night.

[Jon holds out his hand and the razor floats up from the floor back to his hand as he continues shaving, singing The Mole Song as at the beginning]

MOLE SONG (REPRISE)

Every mole could be, potentially
An invitation to the Big C
So get them checked periodically
It could make a difference take it from me.

[He nicks the mole again and drops the razor as at the beginning but this time a phone rings. As the lights switch back on the mirror to blind the audience and Jon 'disappears', we hear a voice:

"Hello, doctor's surgery. Can I help you?"

CURTAIN

Acknowledgements

I nearly didn't include this as the risk of missing anyone out was giving me sleepless nights so let me begin by saying this list is by no means exhaustive. I owe a lot of thanks to a lot of people to have got to where I am today, both in my private and public life. These are the names that are going in this book, if you are not amongst them and are upset that I have not acknowledged your contribution to my life in these pages then please don't tell me. I'll just have more sleepless nights. But I do love you.

My family. Emmah, Nathan and Alfie. We are one of the most dysfunctional family units that I know but how was it ever going to be any other way? We're weird, unique, a little bit crazy and a whole lot of lovely and nothing I do would matter nearly as much if I didn't have you all to take the piss. I love you. Obviously.
My Mum. You're amazing. To get through what has happened over the last few years and still be the person you are today… I will always be proud of you. Thank you and Dad for raising this crazy, creative, PLB!
Jamie Allan. One of a small handful of true friends that I cherish. We don't speak for twenty years and then this. Imagine what we could have done sooner!
Damir Kosutic my consultant at Christie's and all the staff there. Thank you doesn't seem quite adequate but I am certainly thankful that while my speciality is trying to entertain people, yours is saving lives.
Lee Martin, Ollie Downton and the crew at Gag Reflex. Thank you for all your help and guidance. It was a fun time.
Jo Allen. It was an exciting 'journey' through unusual times and I loved that we got to do it together. Thank you for all your hard work.
To the judges, hosts and crew on the world's biggest talent show… what a ride! Thank you for all your kind words and support. It was a blast.
To all my fans, friends and family, even those that didn't vote for me… thank you! (That should cover it.)

Printed in Great Britain
by Amazon